AF688466

Mark Xiornik Rozen Pettinelli Artwork

Check out my artwork online at

cnx.org/content/m63542

and

cnx.org/content/m63475

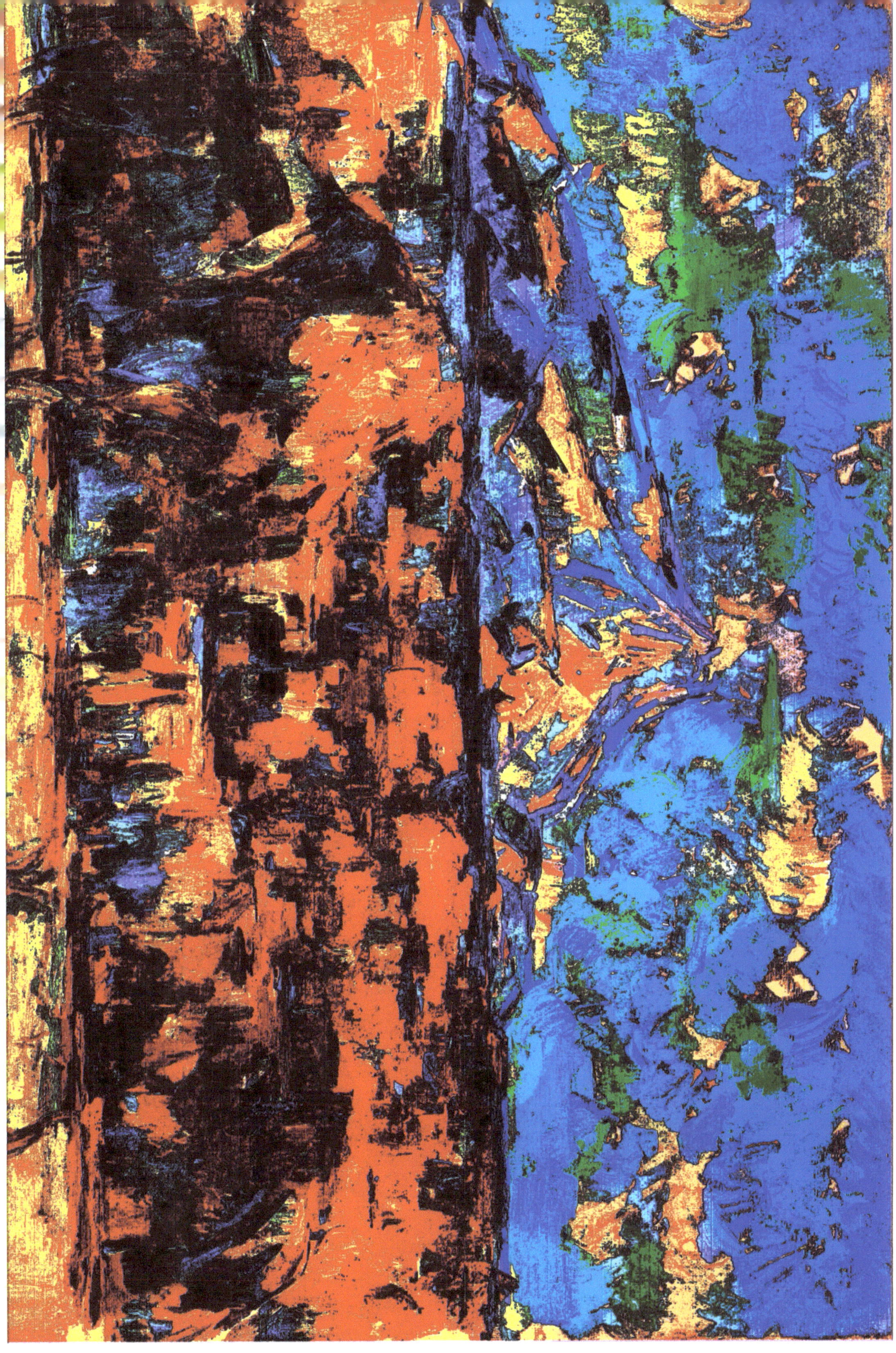

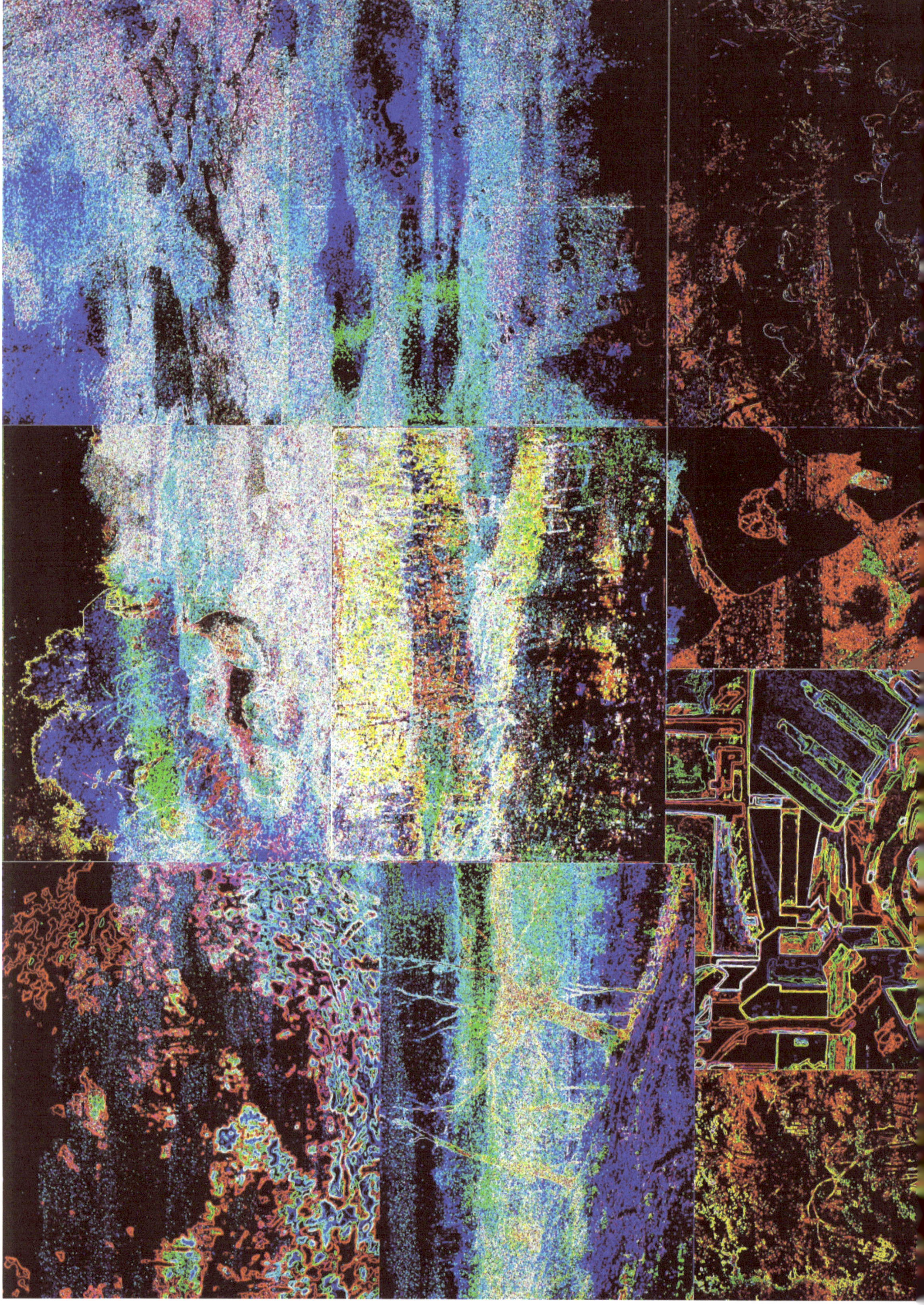

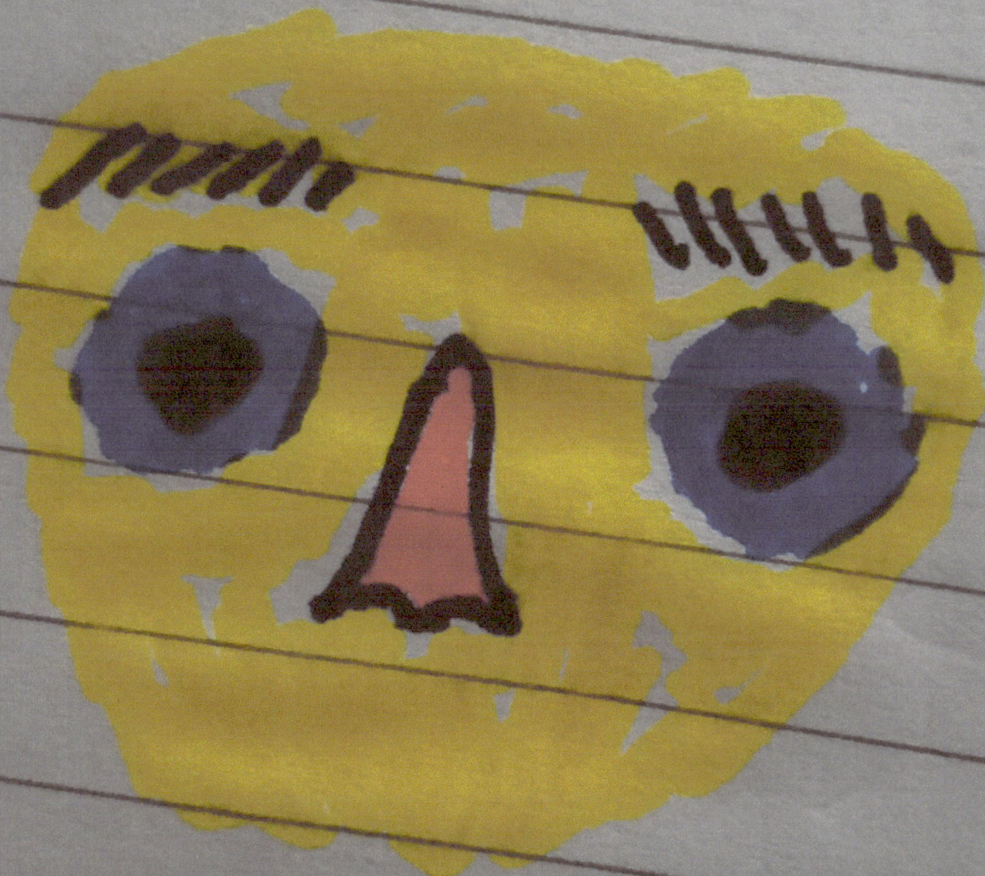

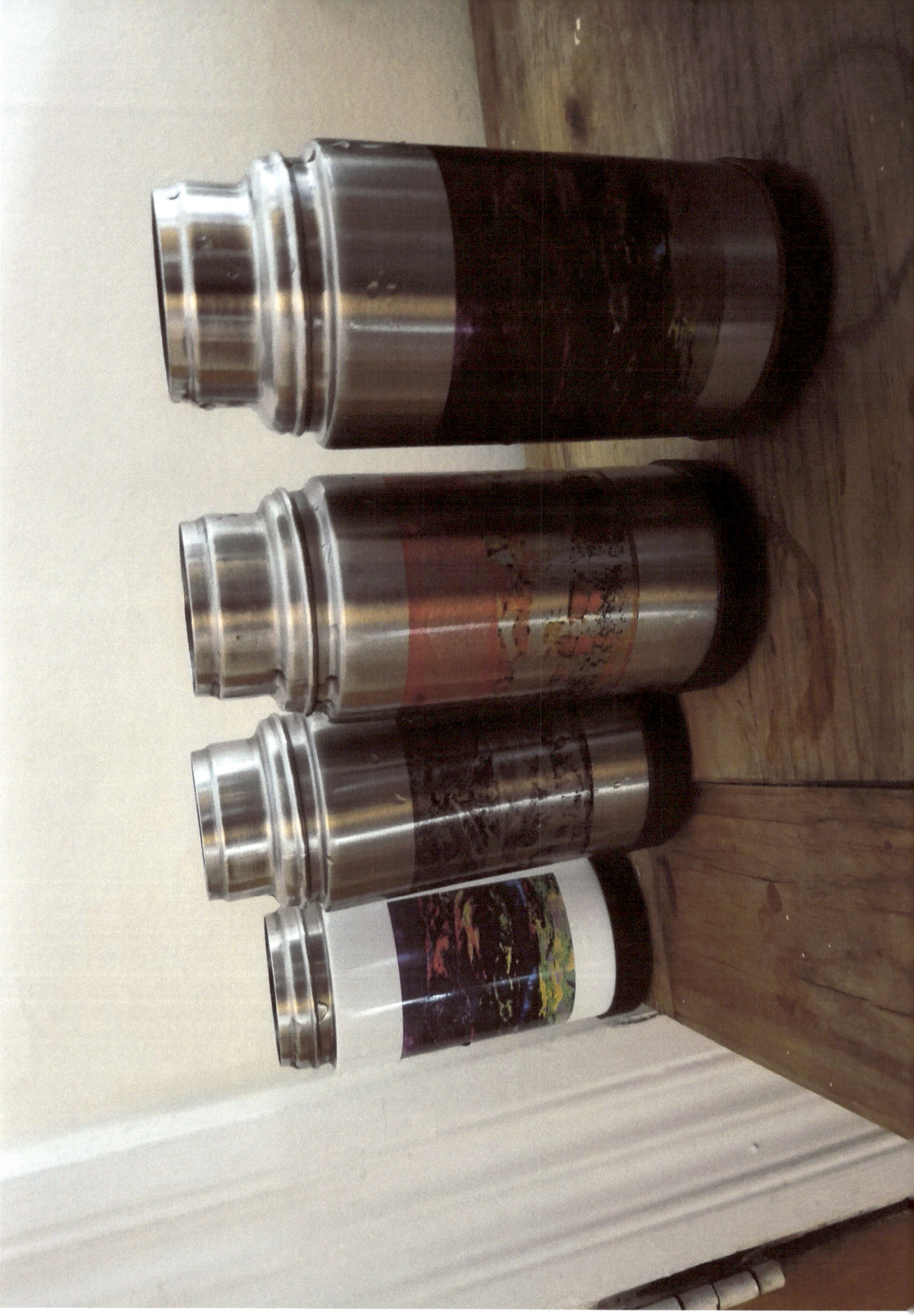

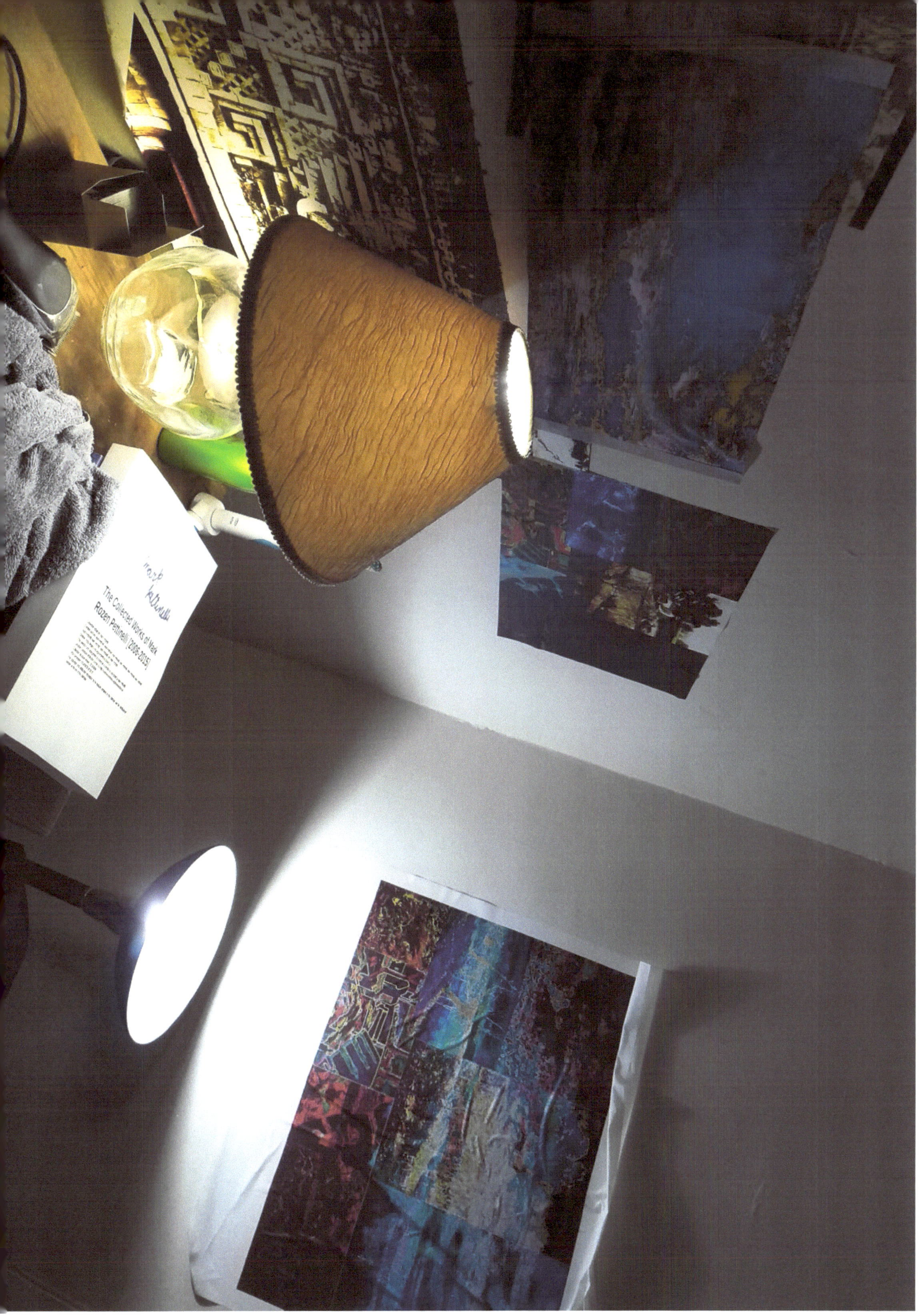
The Collected Works of Mark
Rozen Pettinelli [2006-2015]

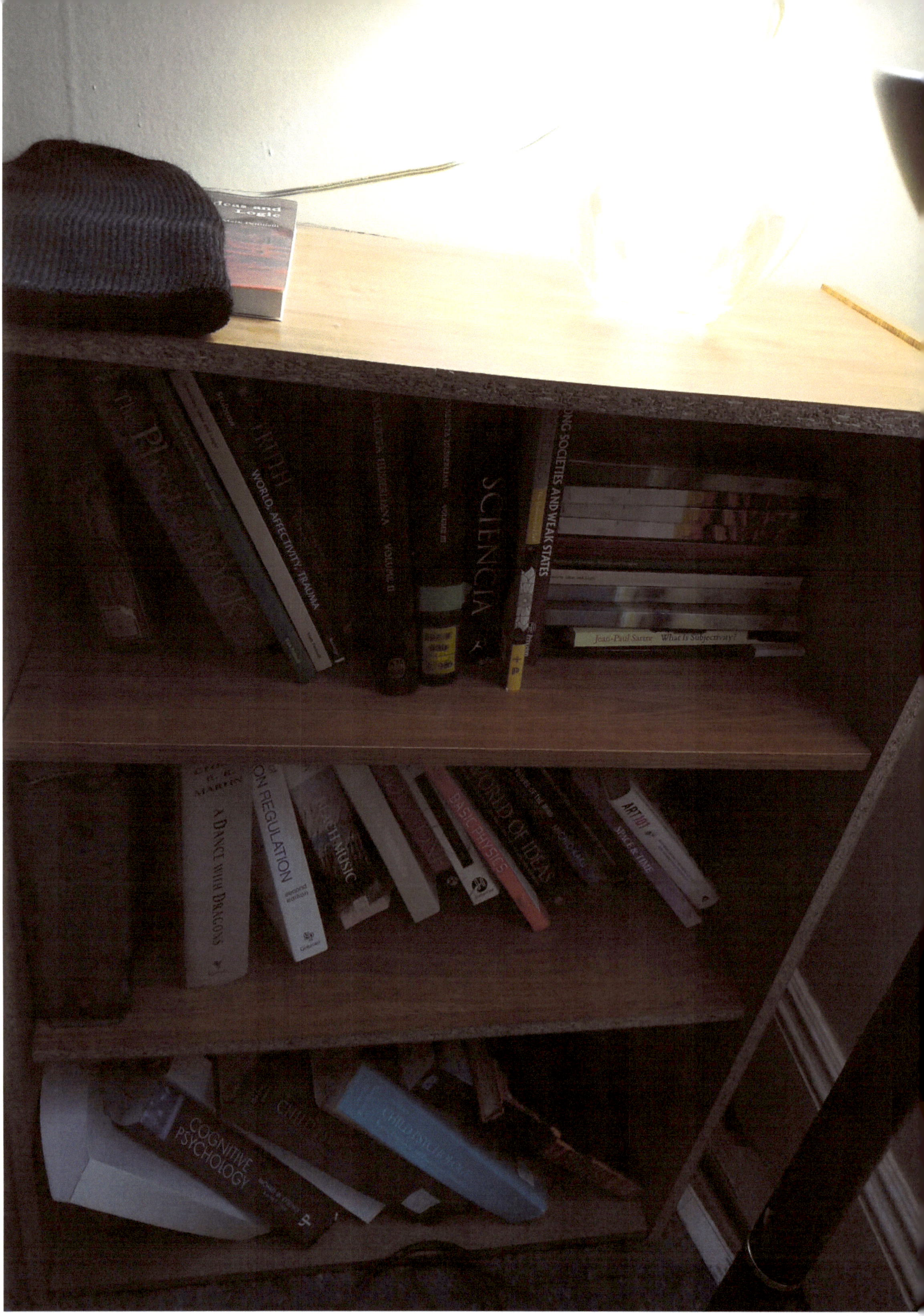
WORLD, AFFECTIVITY, TRAUMA
SCIENCIA
AND WEAK STATES
Jean-Paul Sartre What Is Subjectivity?
A DANCE WITH DRAGONS
BASIC PHYSICS
ART 101
SPACE & TIME
COGNITIVE PSYCHOLOGY

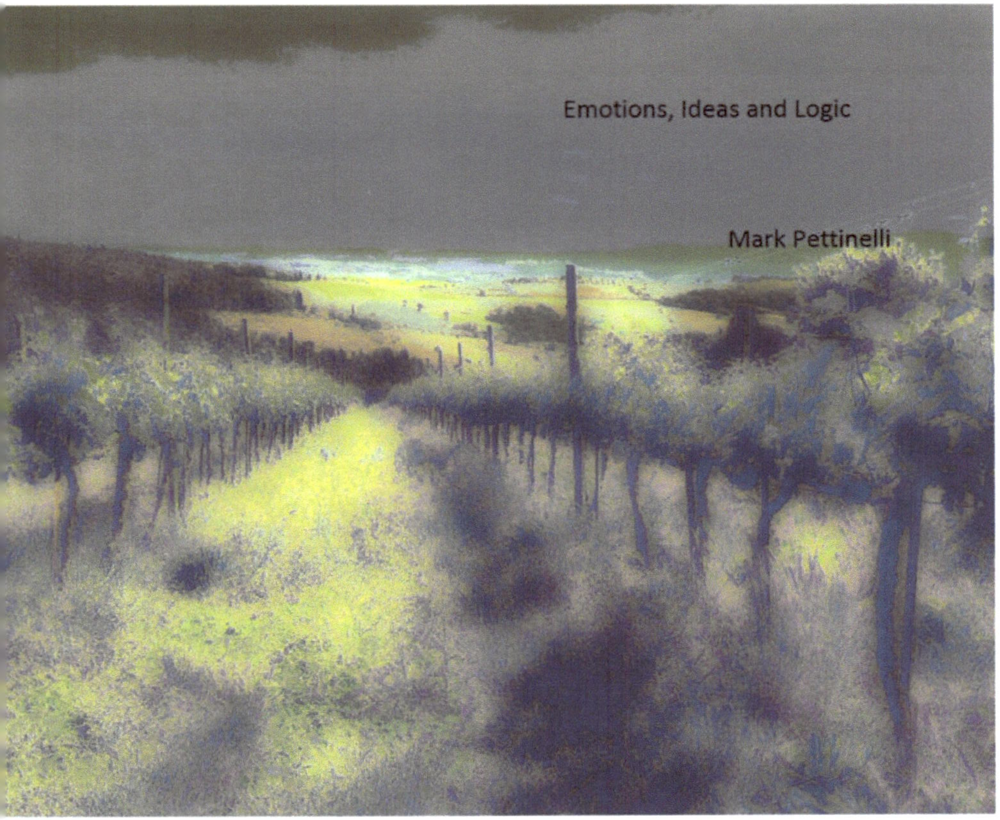

The Collected Works of Mark Rozen Pettinelli [2006-2015]

Collection edited by: Mark Pettinelli
Content authors: Mark Pettinelli, Mark Pettinelli, Mark Pettinelli, Mark Pettinelli, Mark Pettinelli, Mark Pettinelli, Mark Pettinelli, Mark Pettinelli, Mark Pettinelli, and Mark Pettinelli
Online: <http://legacy.cnx.org/content/col12044/1.1>

Collection structure revised: 2016/08/09
PDF Generated: 2016/08/09 08:58:05

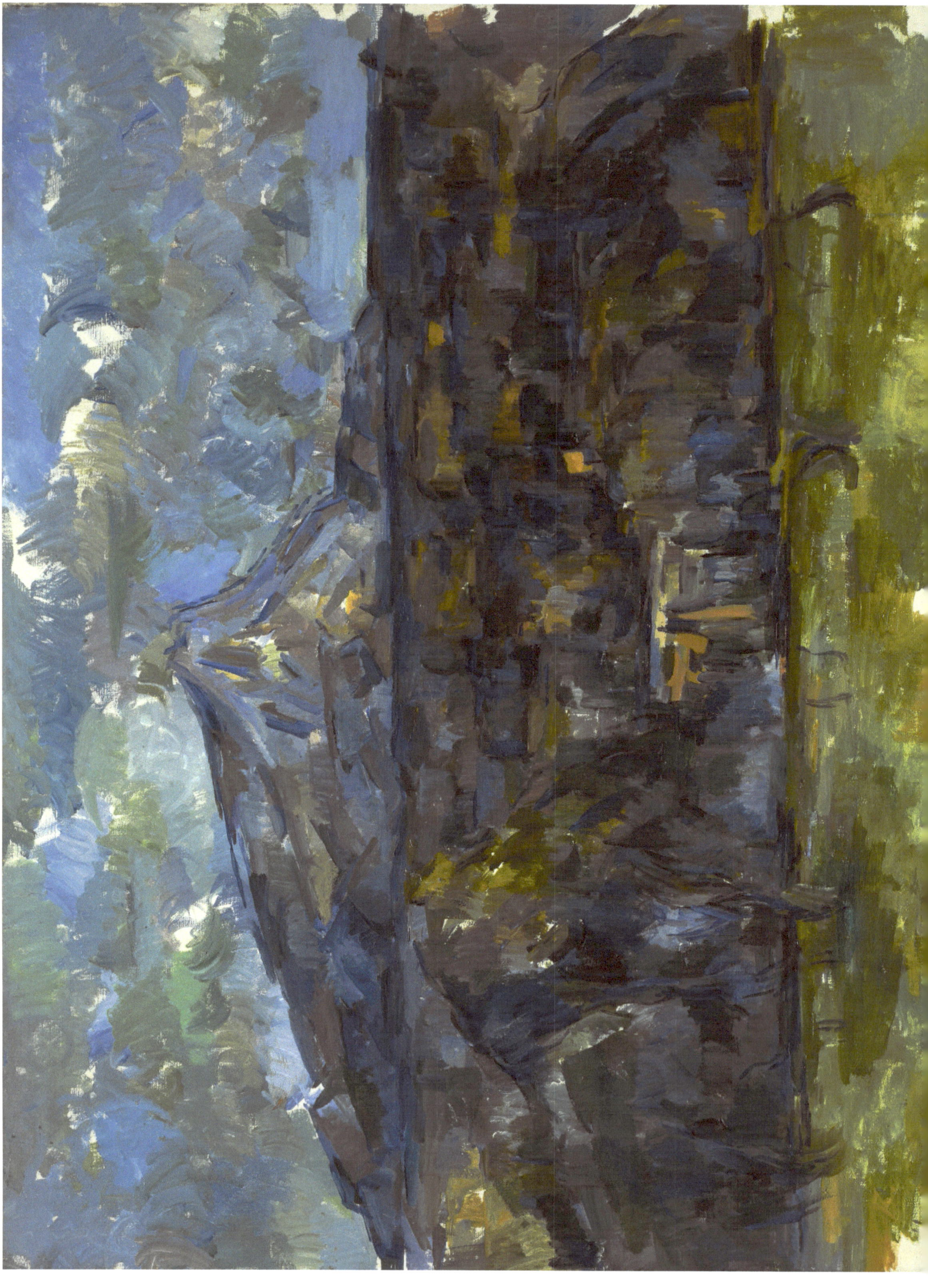

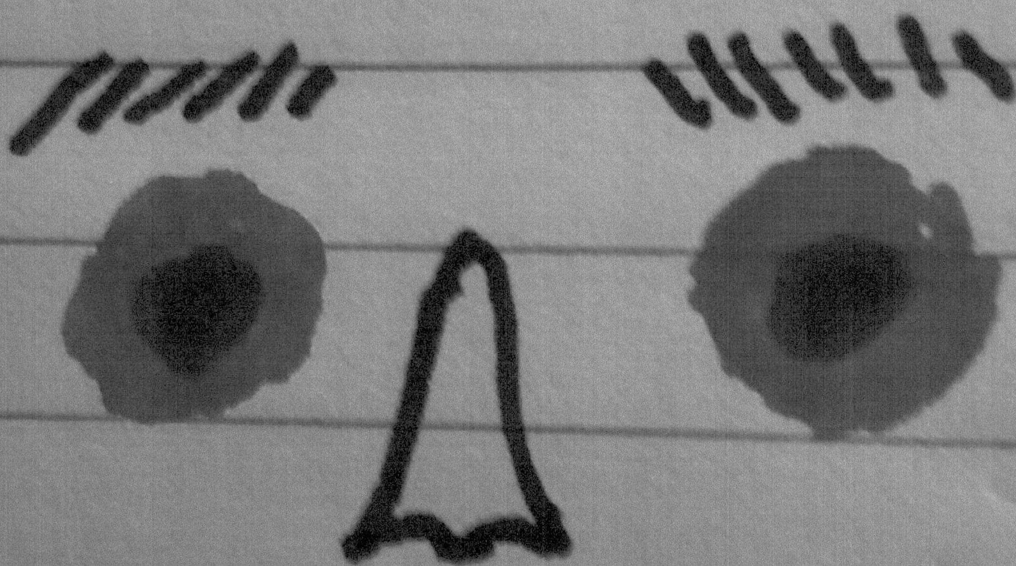

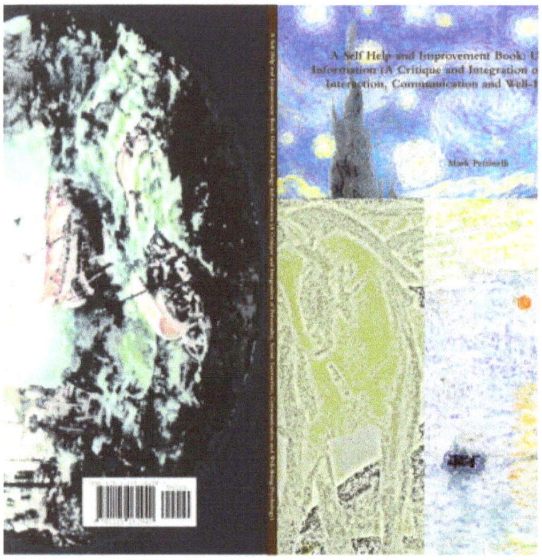

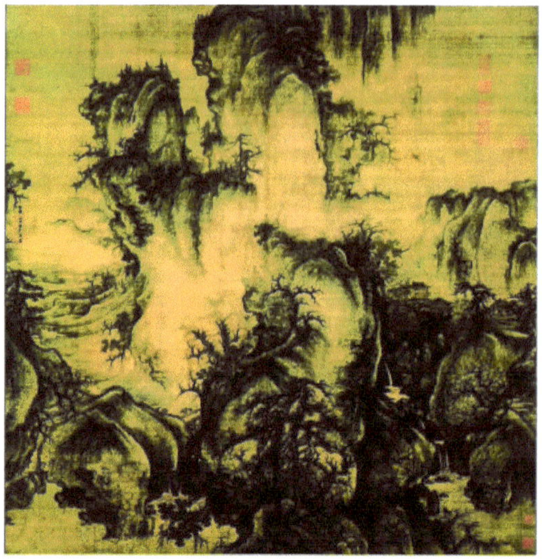

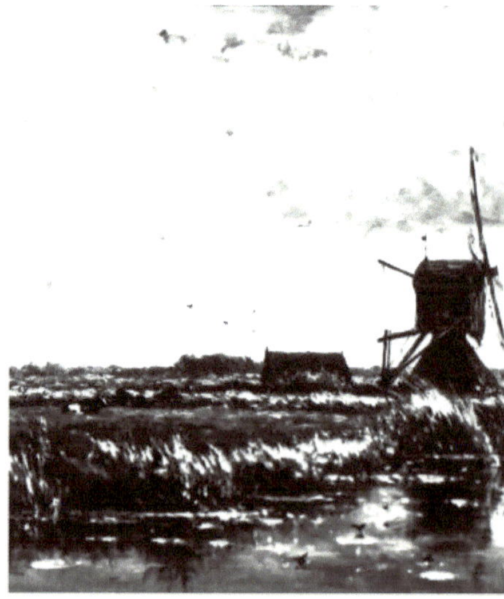

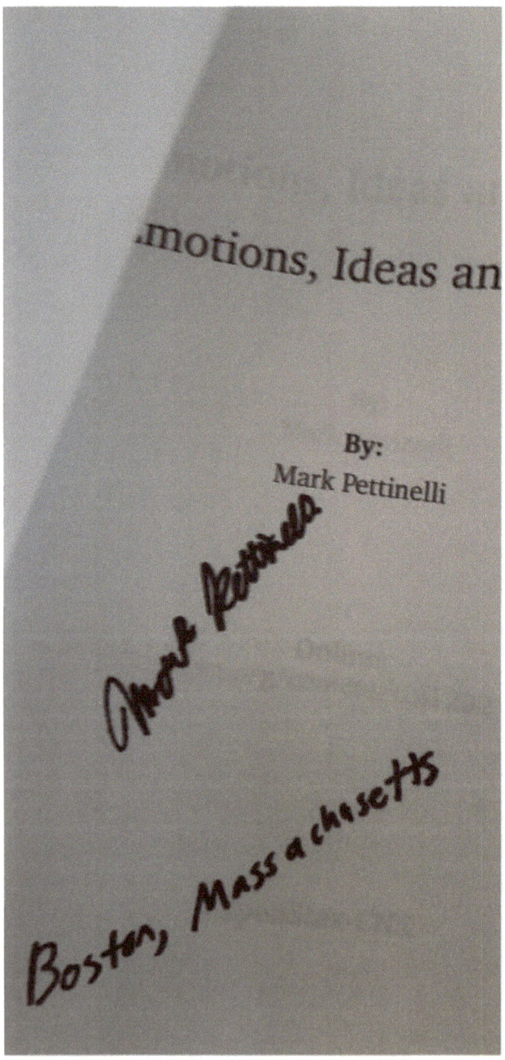
By:
Mark Pettinelli
Mark Pettinelli
Boston, Massachusetts

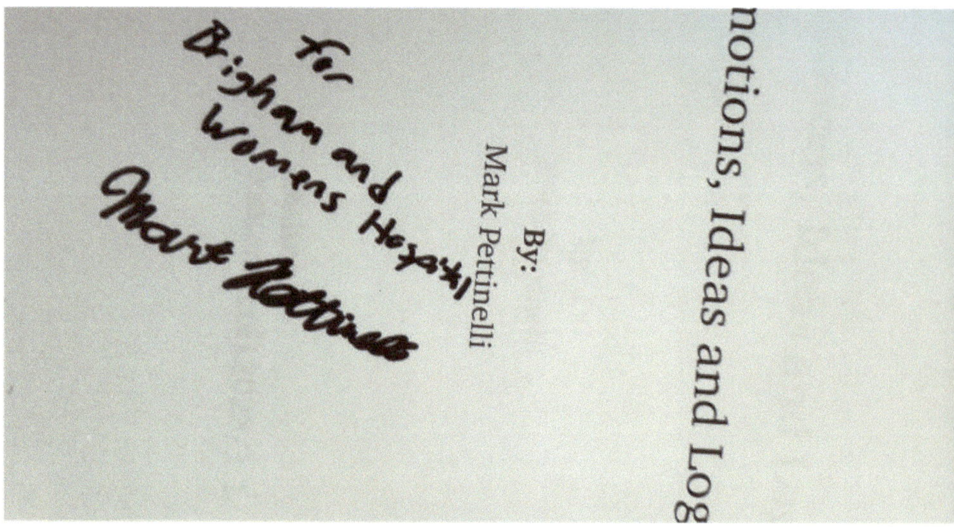
for
Brigham and
Womens Hospital
Mark Pettinelli
By:
Mark Pettinelli

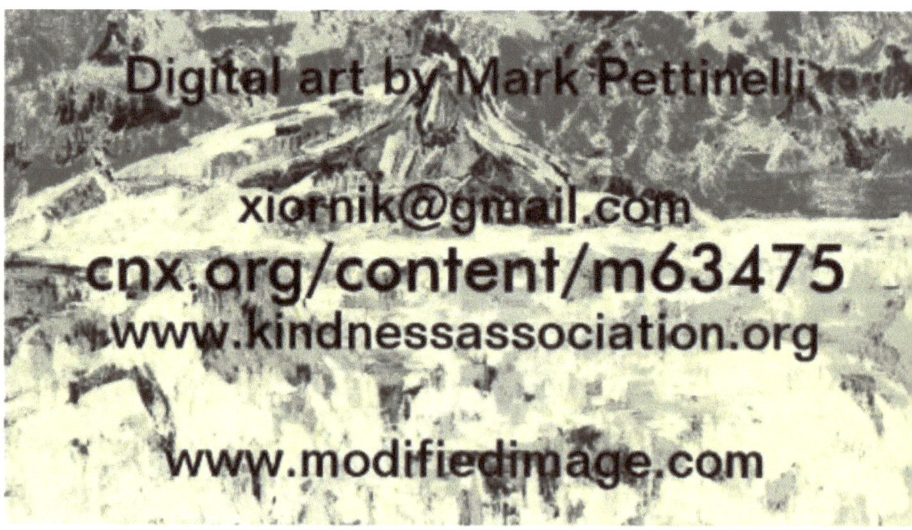
Digital art by Mark Pettinelli
xiornik@gmail.com
cnx.org/content/m63475
www.kindnessassociation.org
www.modifiedimage.com

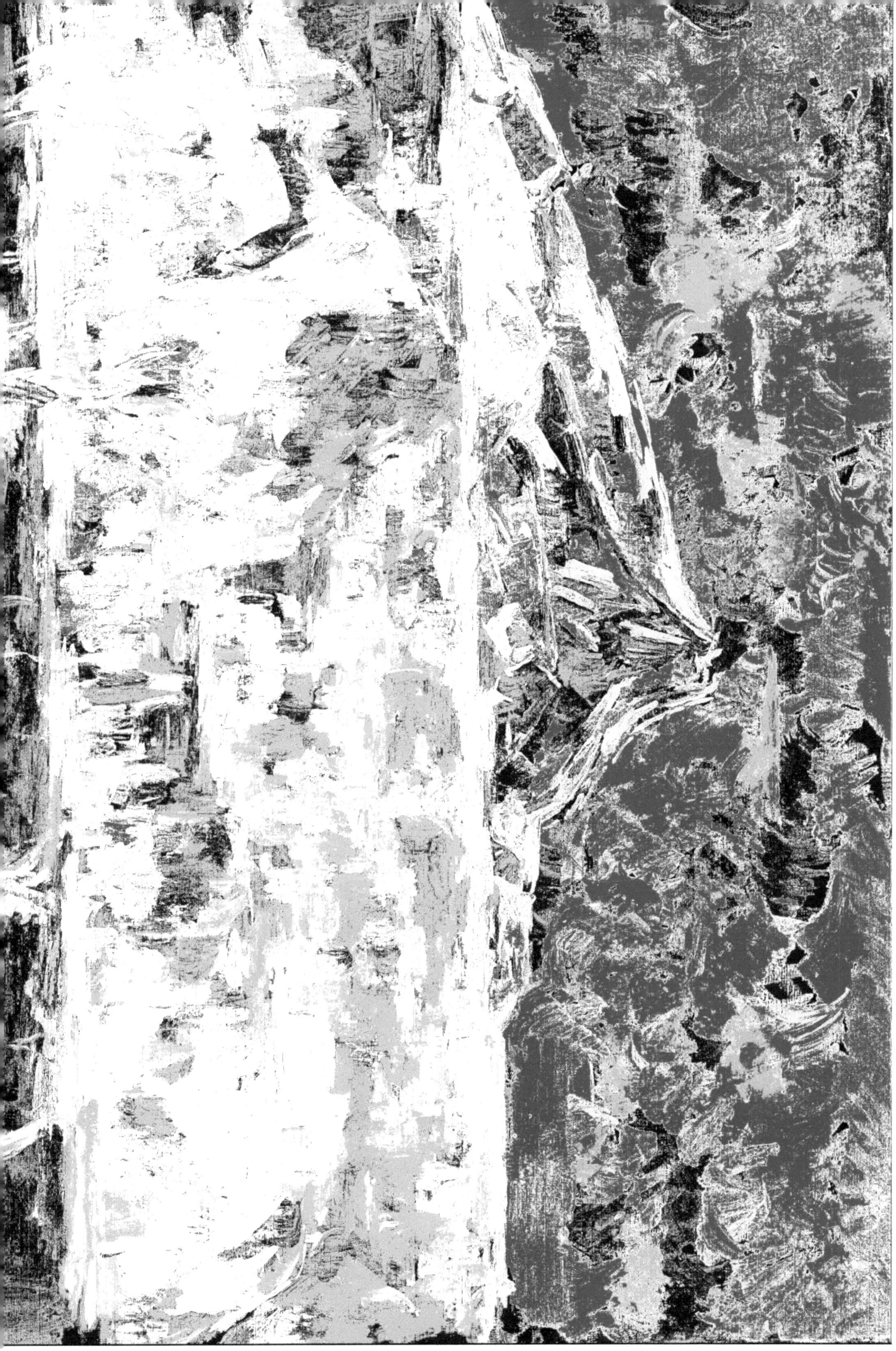

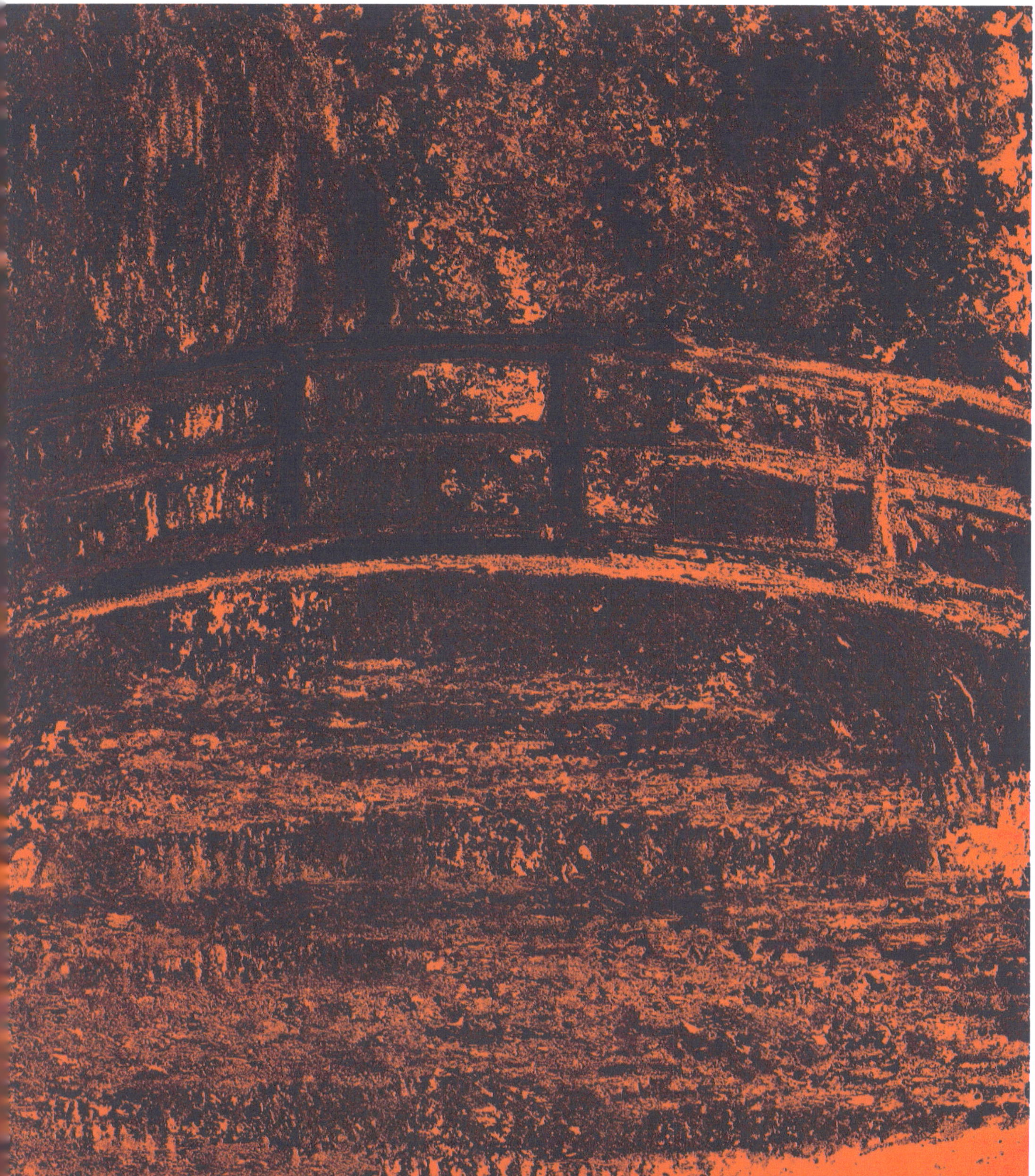

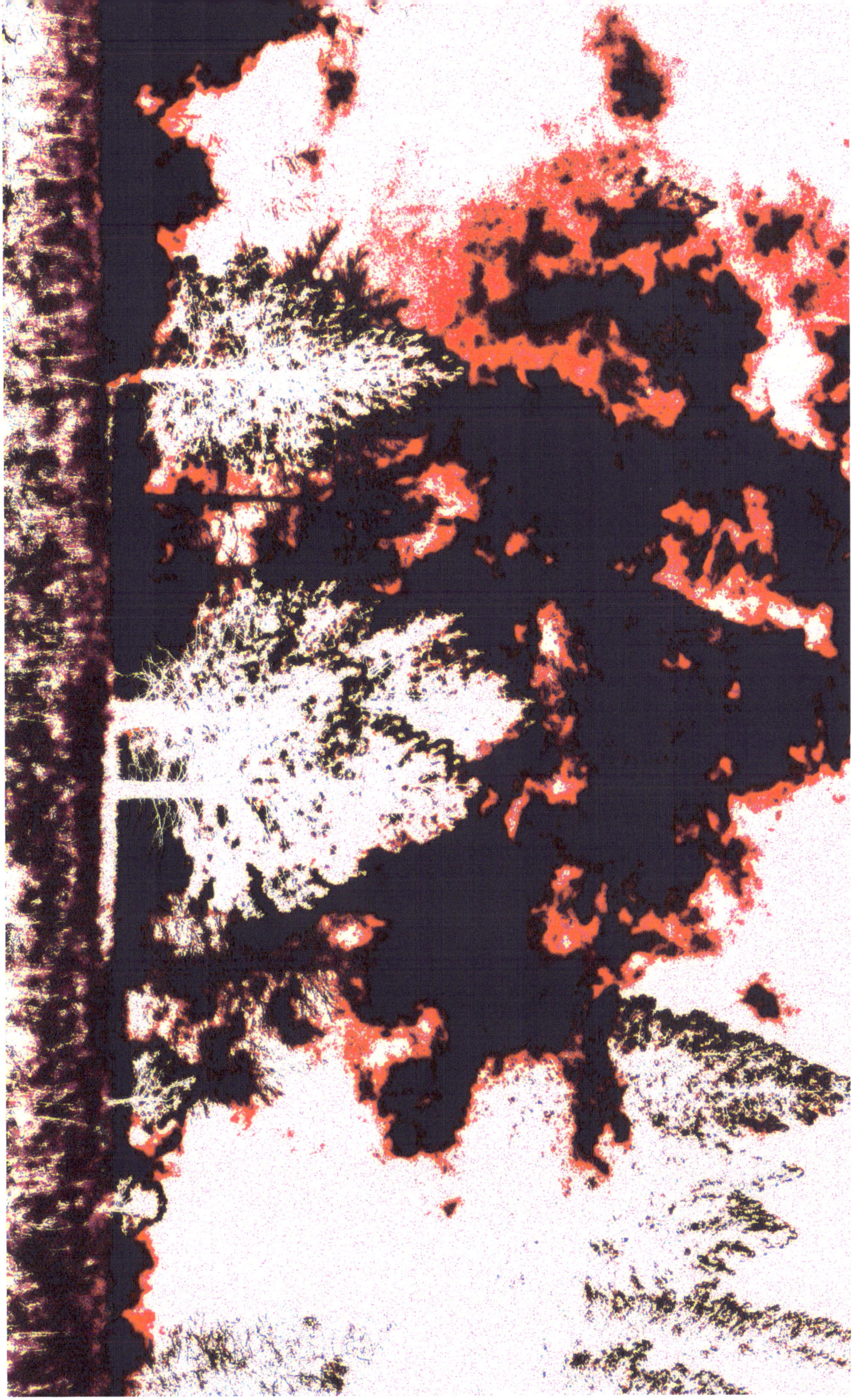

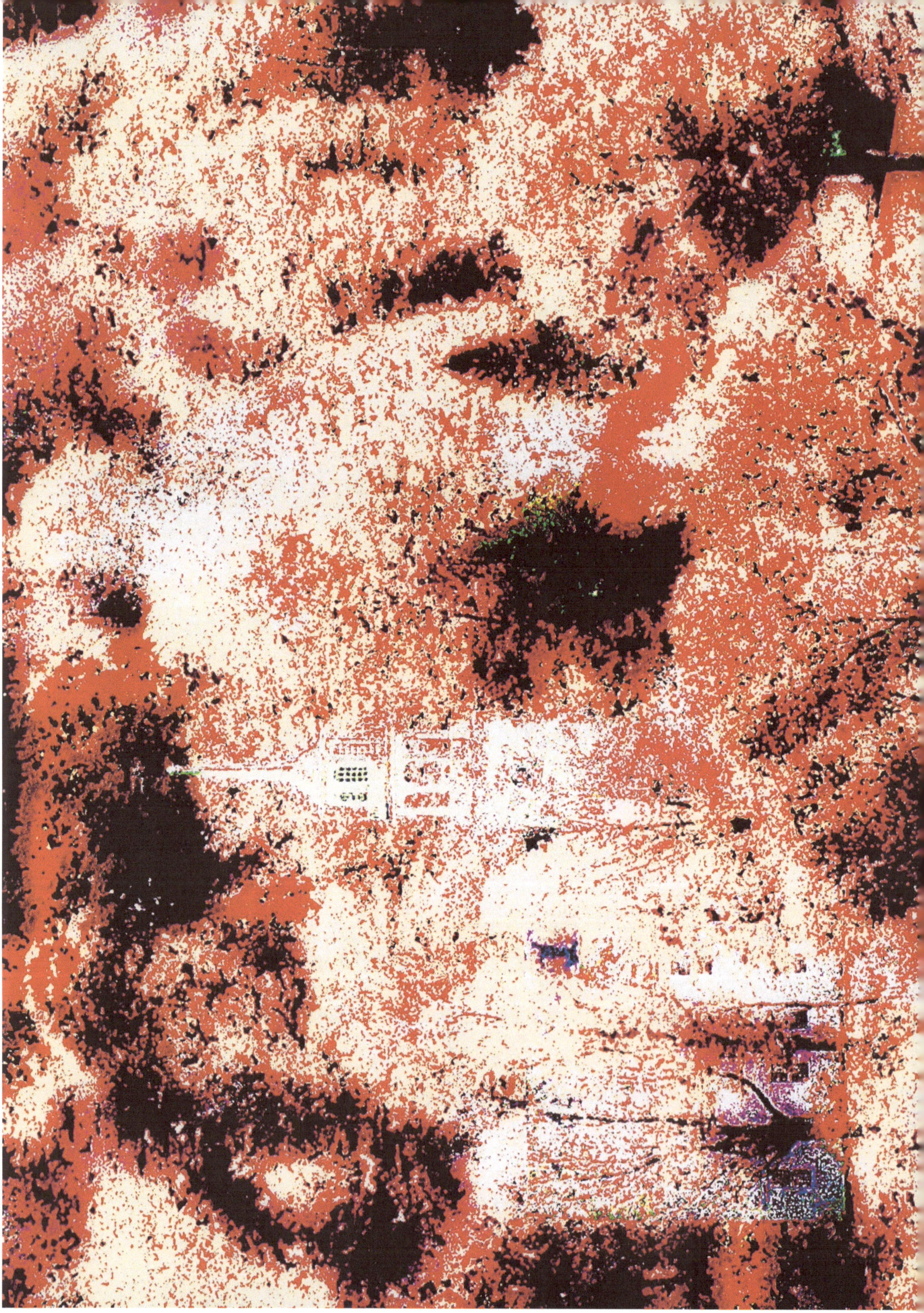

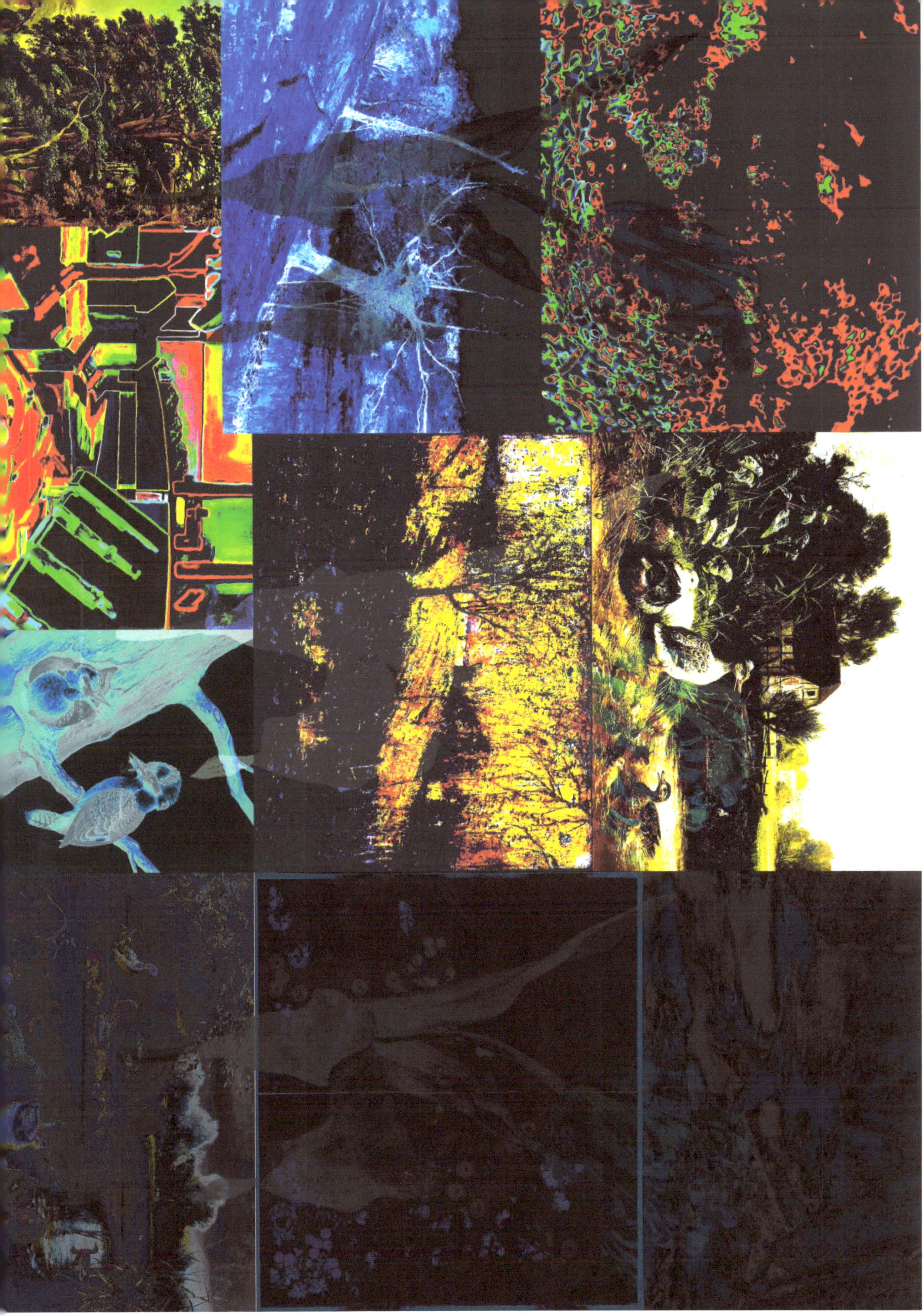

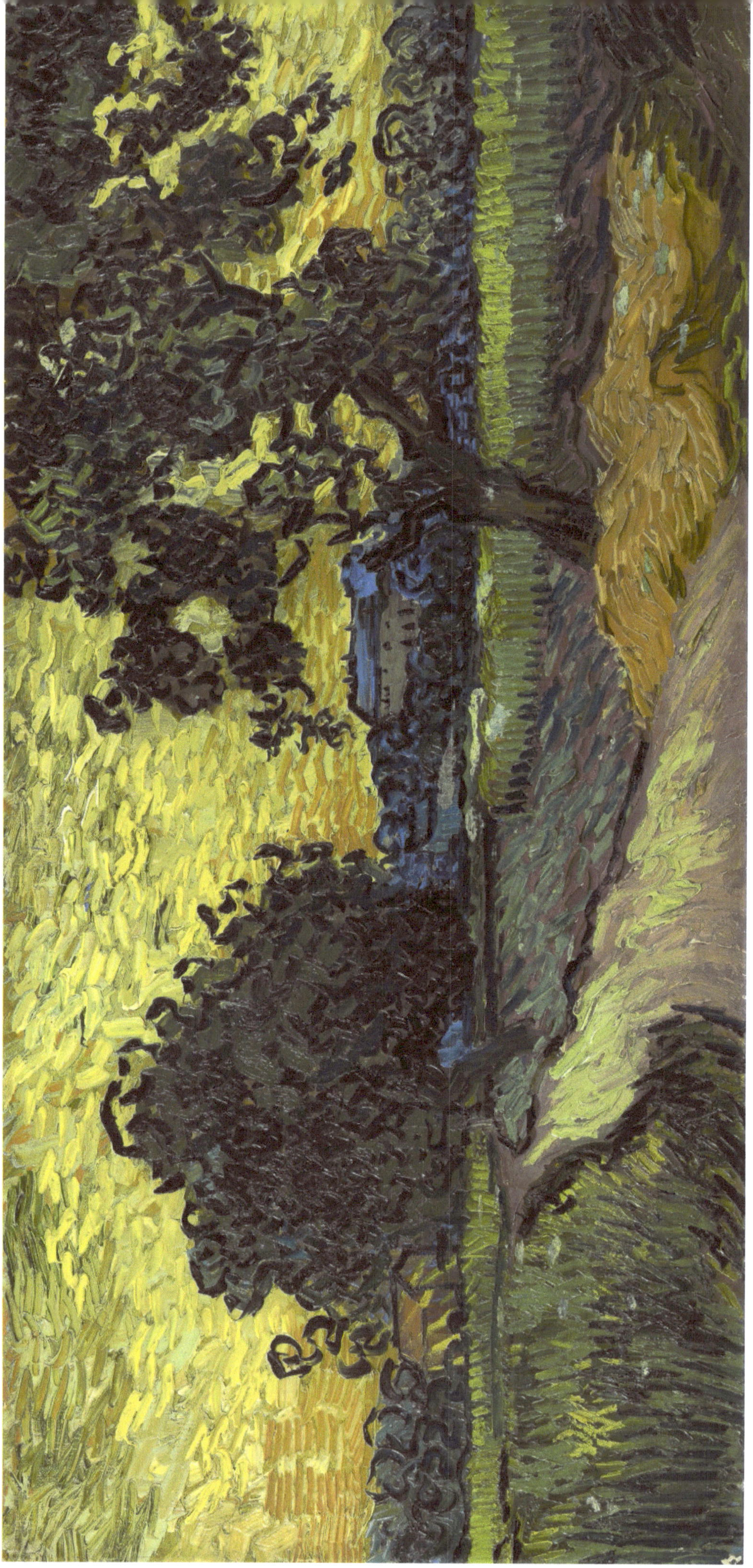

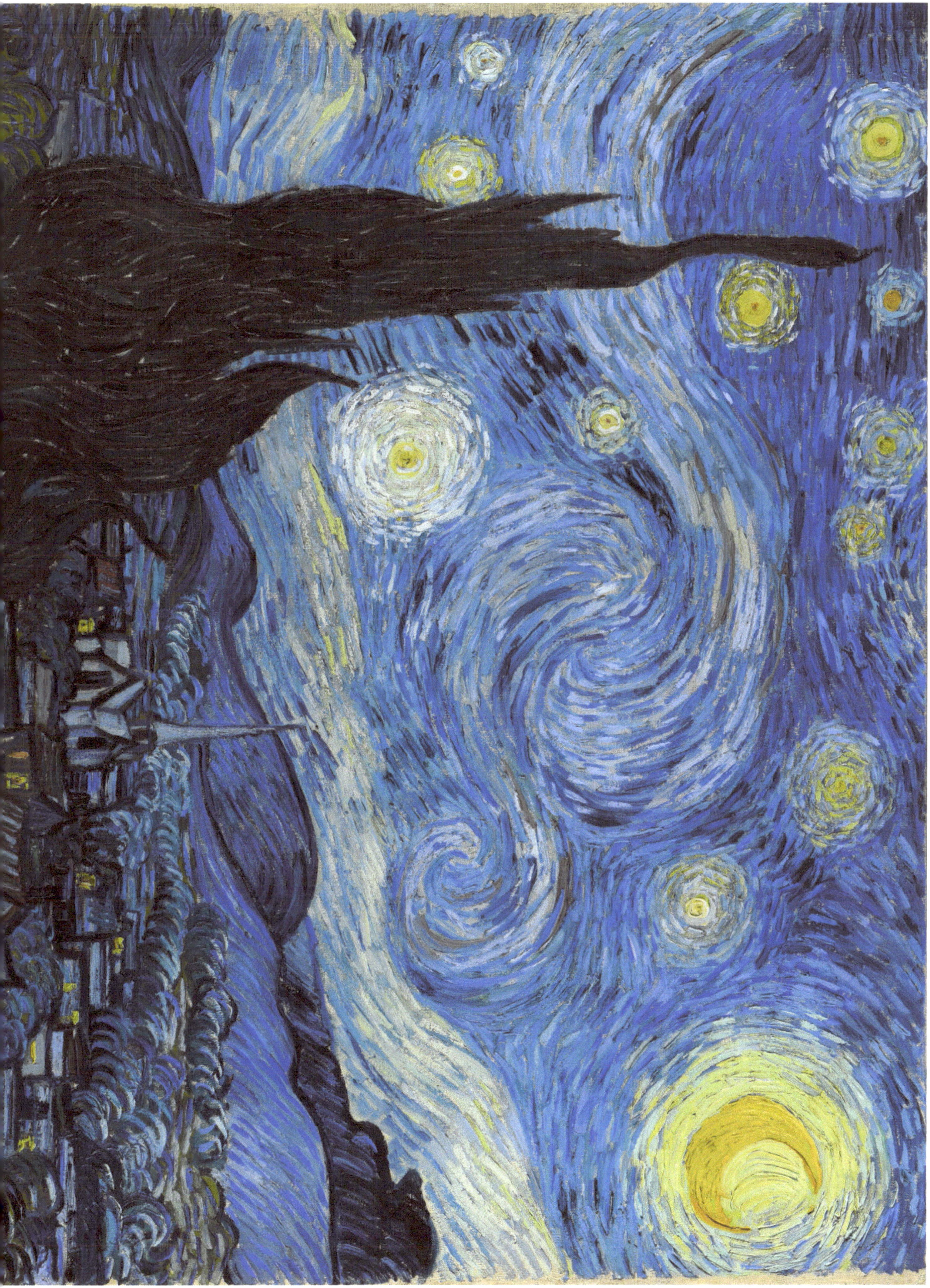

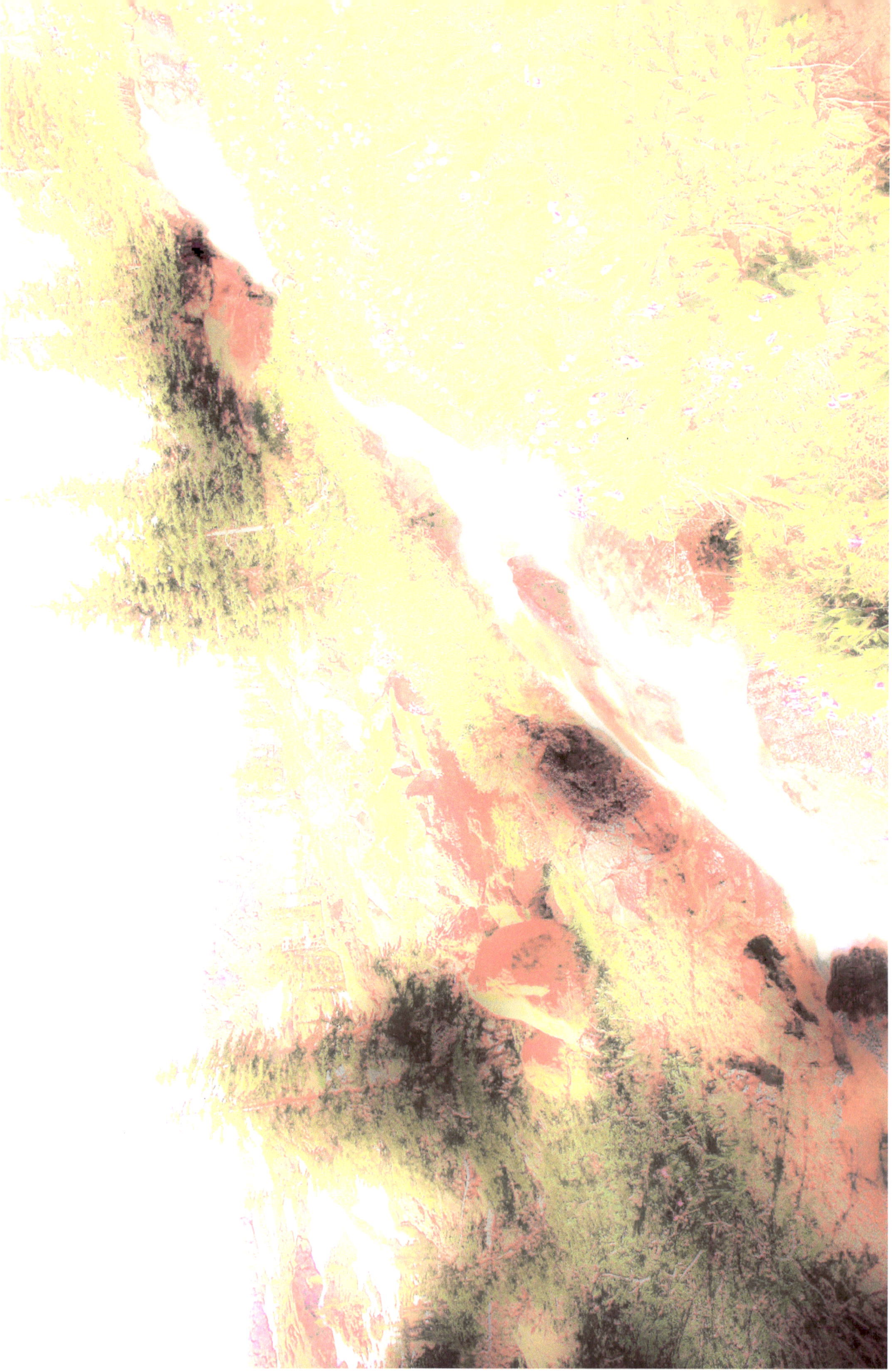

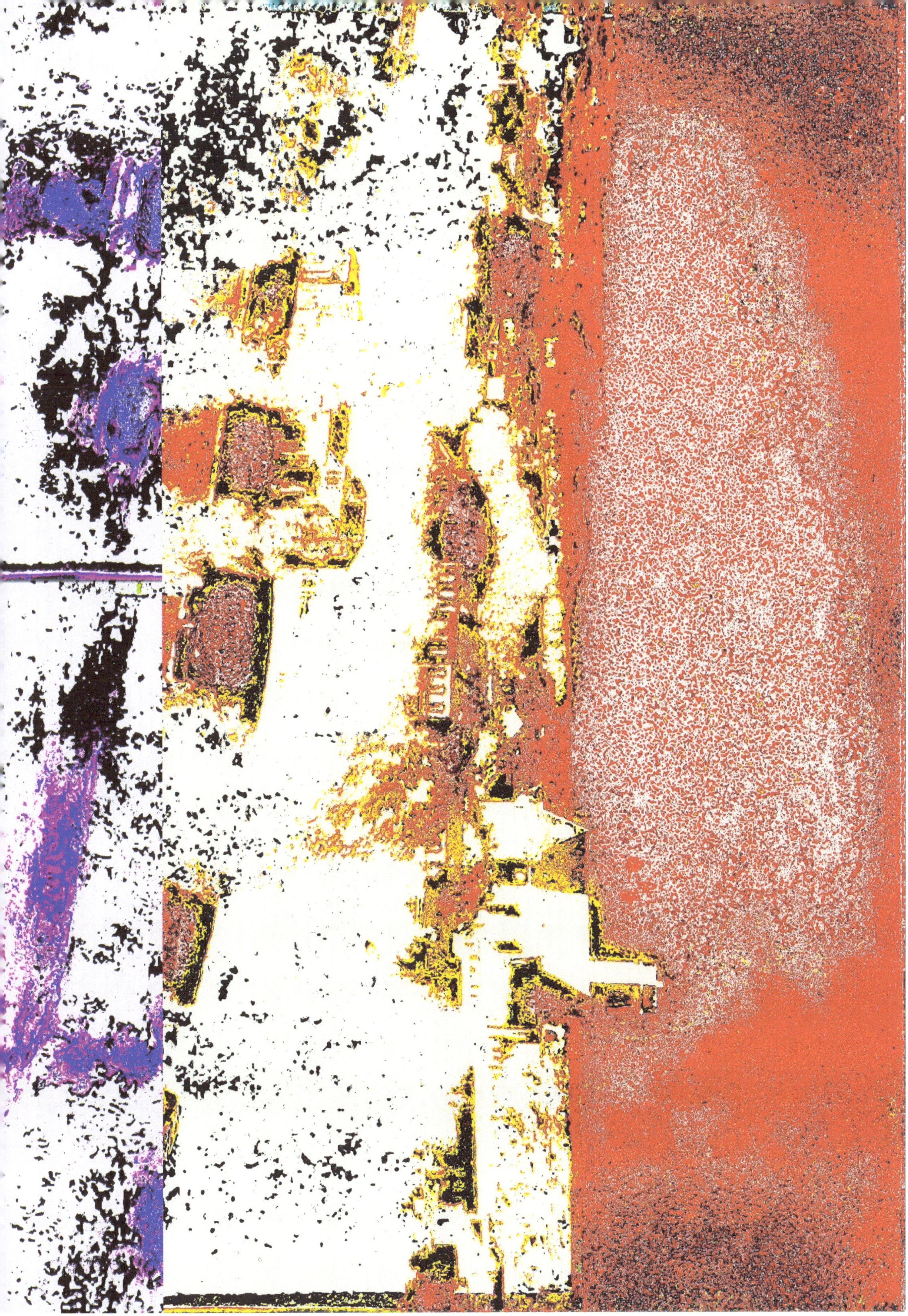

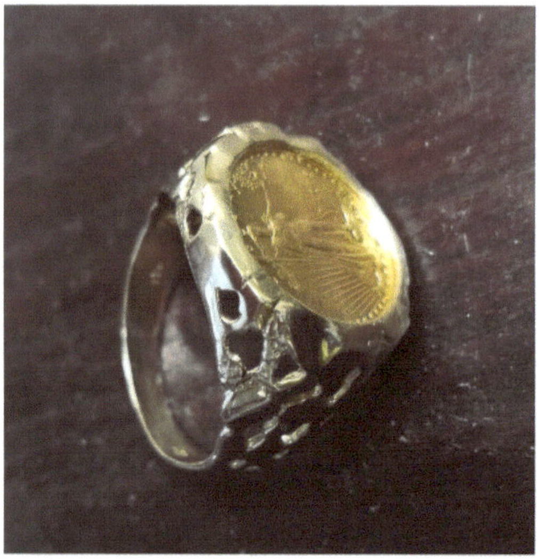
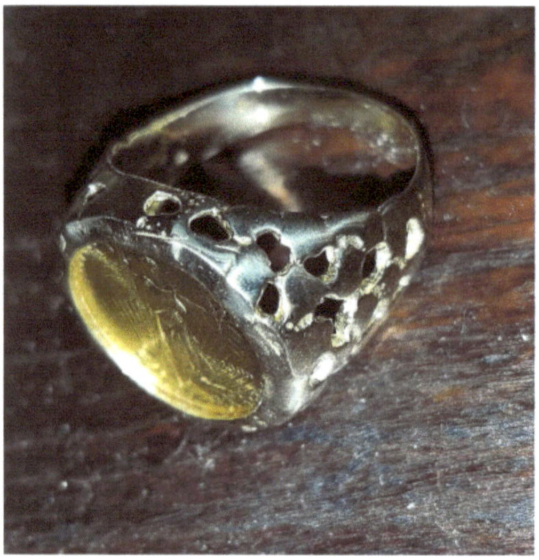
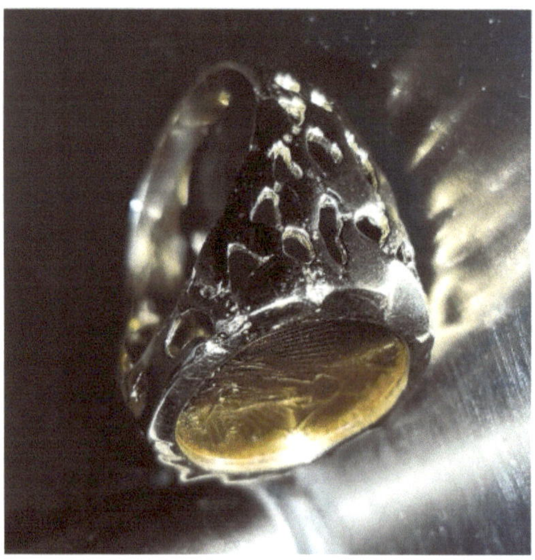
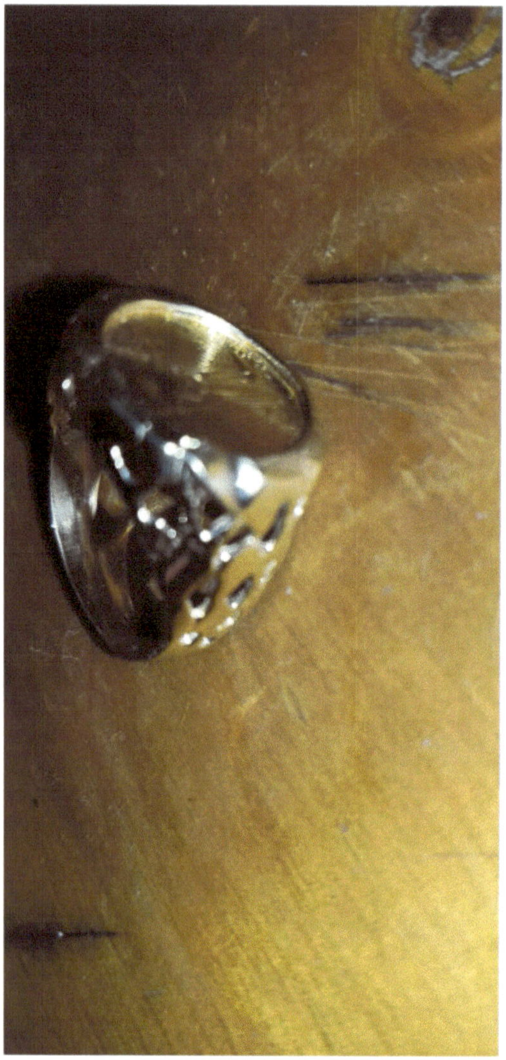
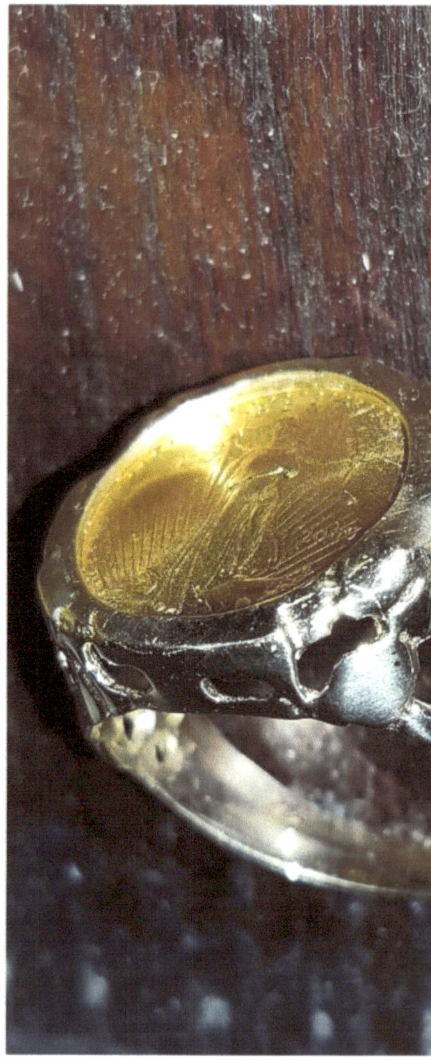
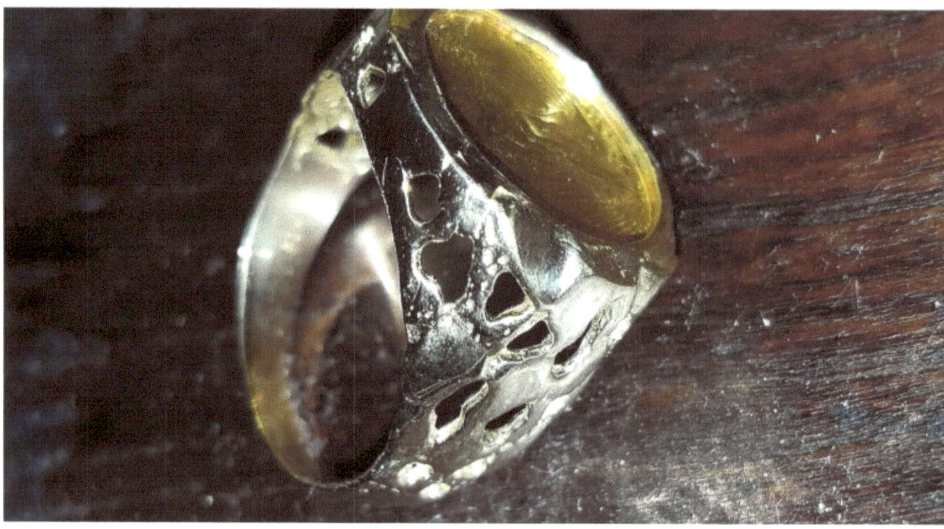

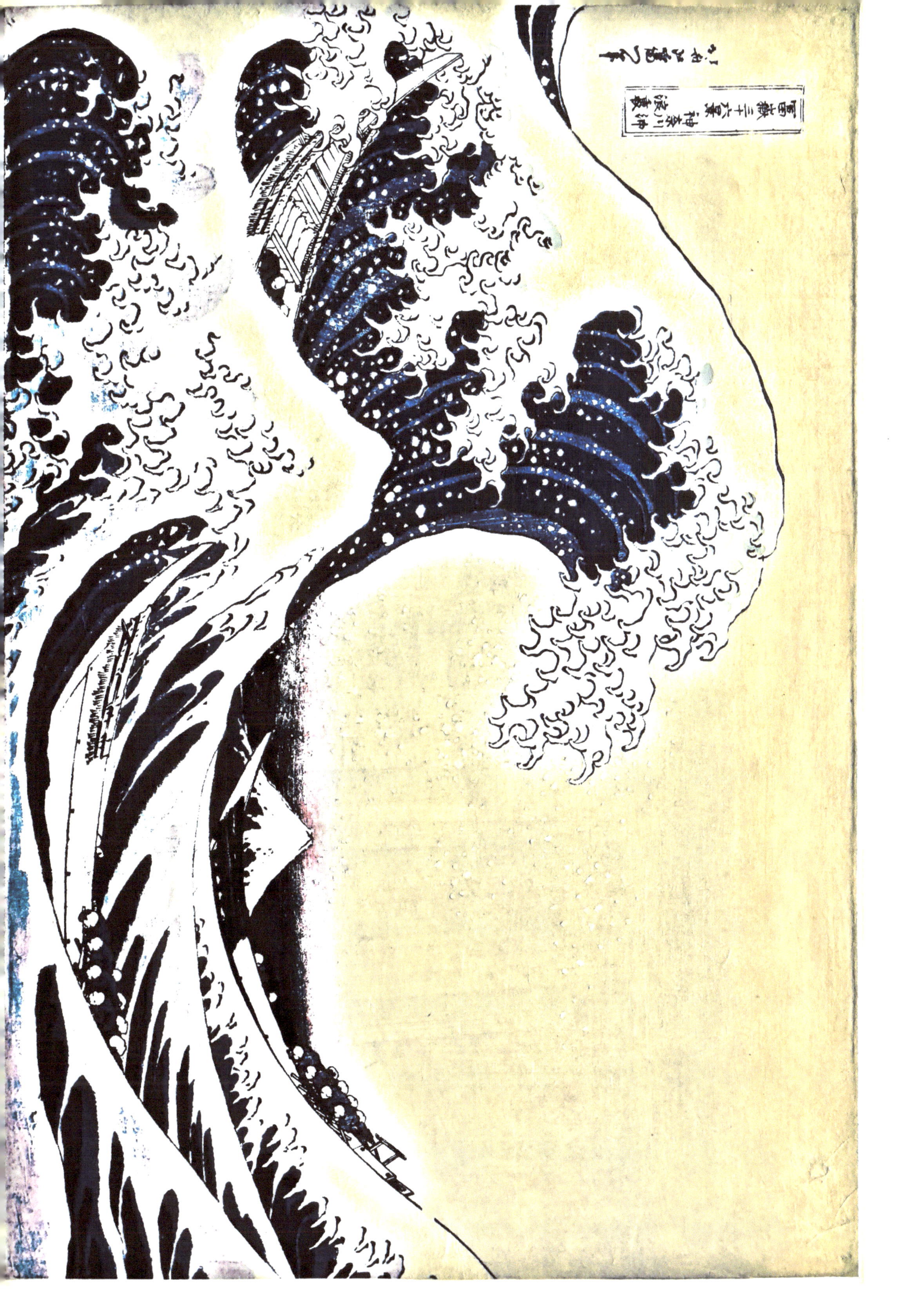

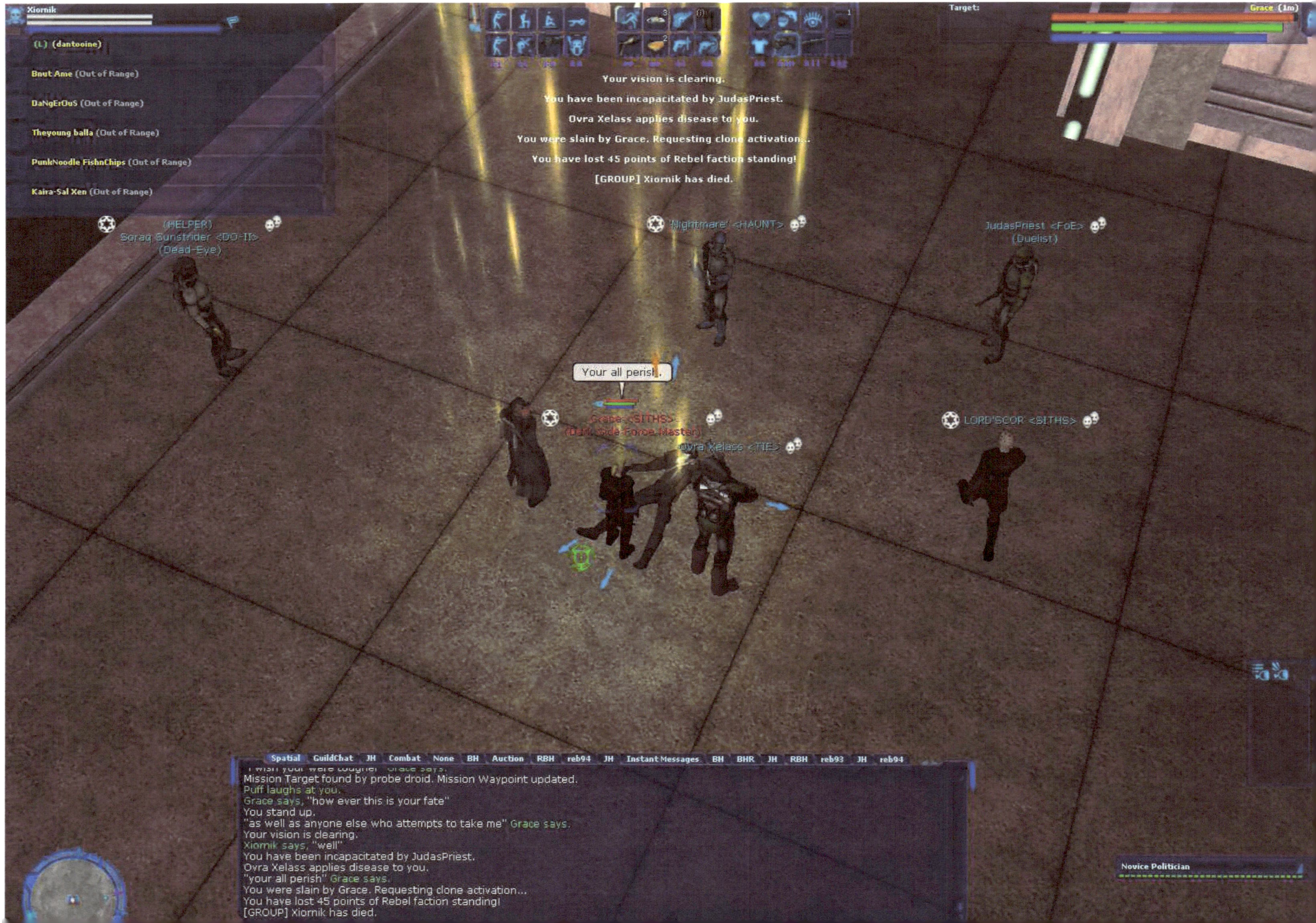
Xiornik
(L) (dantooine)
Bnut Ame (Out of Range)
DaNgErOuS (Out of Range)
Theyoung balla (Out of Range)
PunkNoodle FishnChips (Out of Range)
Kaira-Sal Xen (Out of Range)
Target:
Grace (1m)
Your vision is clearing.
You have been incapacitated by JudasPriest.
Ovra Xelass applies disease to you.
You were slain by Grace. Requesting clone activation...
You have lost 45 points of Rebel faction standing!
[GROUP] Xiornik has died.
(HELPER)
Soraq Sunstrider <DO-II>
(Dead-Eye)
'Nightmare' <HAUNT>
JudasPriest <FoE>
(Duelist)
Your all perish.
Grace <SITHS>
LORD'SCOR <SITHS>
Ovra Xelass <TIE>
Spatial GuildChat JH Combat None BH Auction RBH reb94 JH Instant Messages BH BHR JH RBH reb93 JH reb94
Mission Target found by probe droid. Mission Waypoint updated.
Puff laughs at you.
Grace says, "how ever this is your fate"
You stand up.
"as well as anyone else who attempts to take me" Grace says.
Your vision is clearing.
Xiornik says, "well"
You have been incapacitated by JudasPriest.
Ovra Xelass applies disease to you.
"your all perish" Grace says.
You were slain by Grace. Requesting clone activation...
You have lost 45 points of Rebel faction standing!
[GROUP] Xiornik has died.
Novice Politician

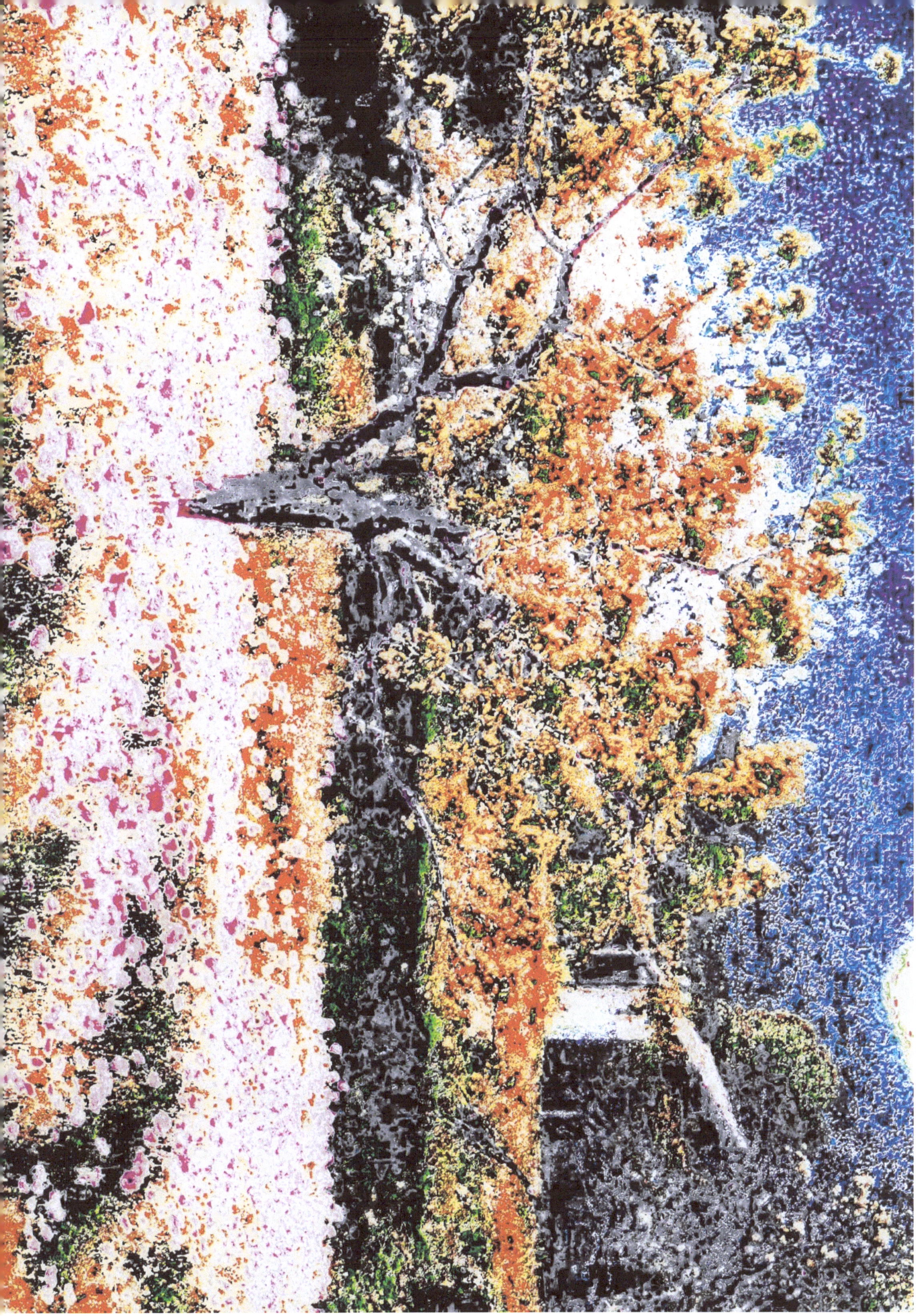

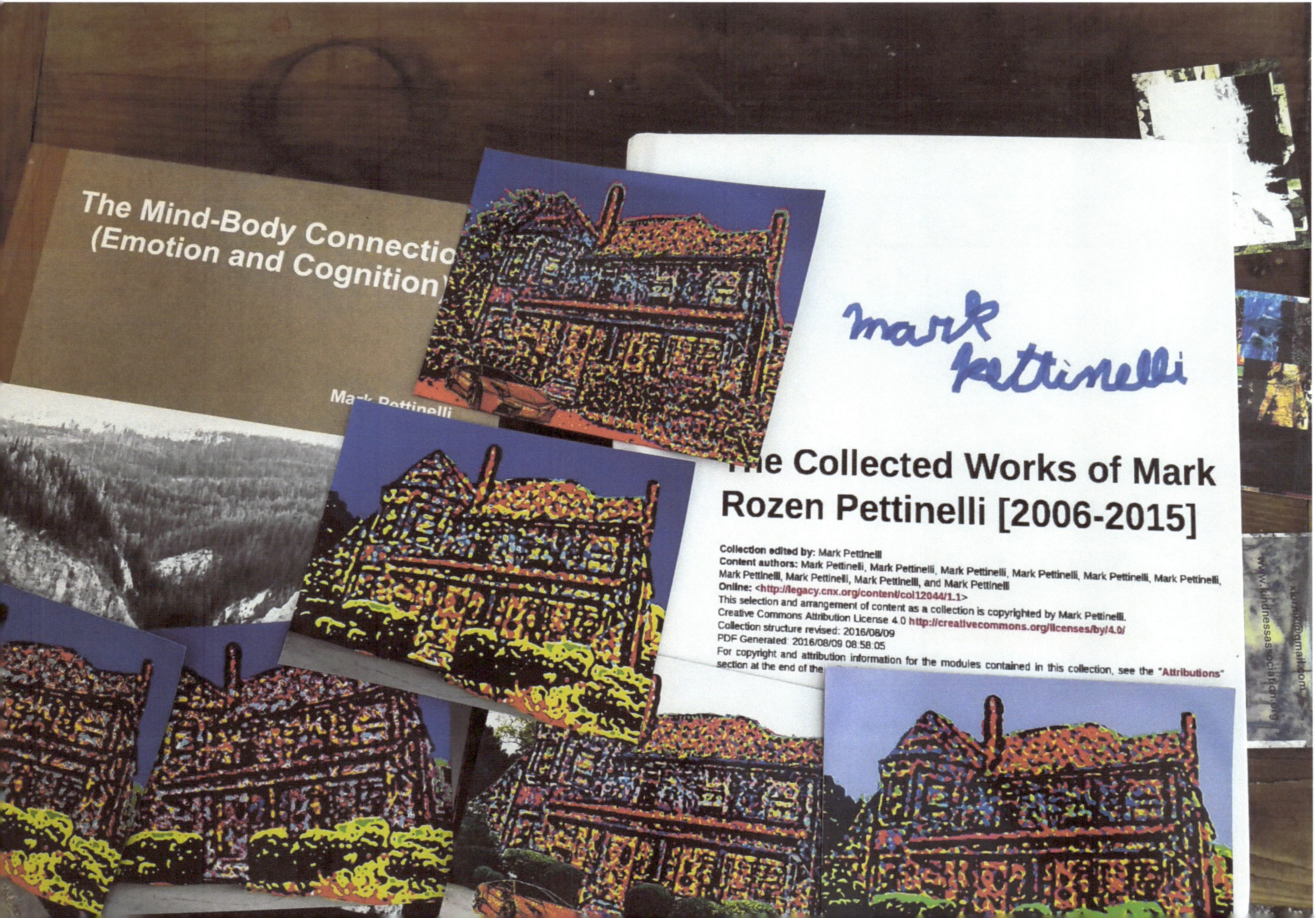
The Mind-Body Connectio
(Emotion and Cognition)
mark pettinelli
e Collected Works of Mark
Rozen Pettinelli [2006-2015]
Collection edited by: Mark Pettinelli
Content authors: Mark Pettinelli, Mark Pettinelli, Mark Pettinelli, Mark Pettinelli, Mark Pettinelli, Mark Pettinelli, Mark Pettinelli, Mark Pettinelli, Mark Pettinelli, and Mark Pettinelli
Online: <http://legacy.cnx.org/content/col12044/1.1>
This selection and arrangement of content as a collection is copyrighted by Mark Pettinelli.
Creative Commons Attribution License 4.0 http://creativecommons.org/licenses/by/4.0/
Collection structure revised: 2016/08/09
PDF Generated: 2016/08/09 08:58:05
For copyright and attribution information for the modules contained in this collection, see the "Attributions"
section at the end of the
www.kindnessassociation.org

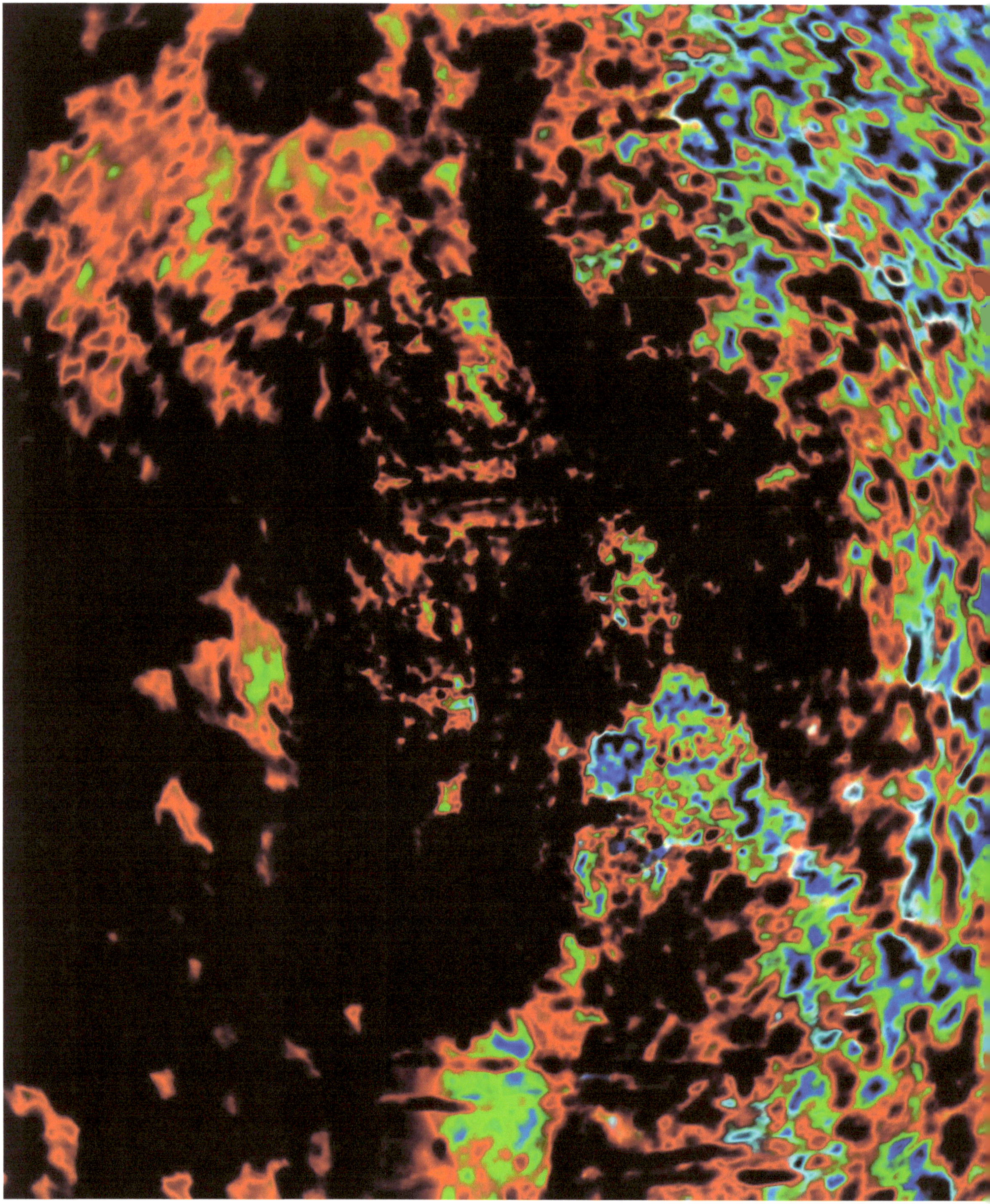

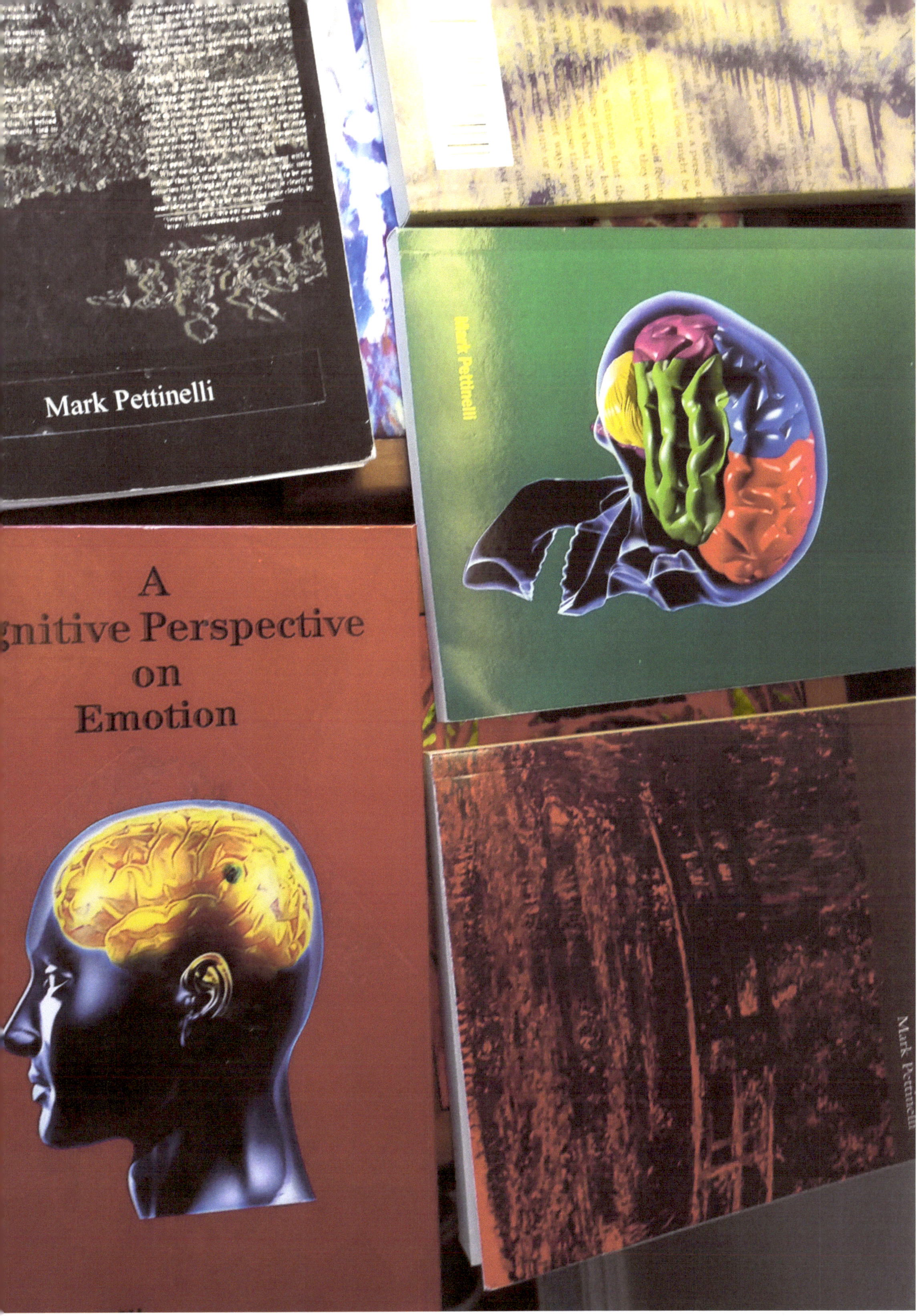
Mark Pettinelli
Mark Pettinelli
A
gnitive Perspective
on
Emotion
Mark Pettinelli

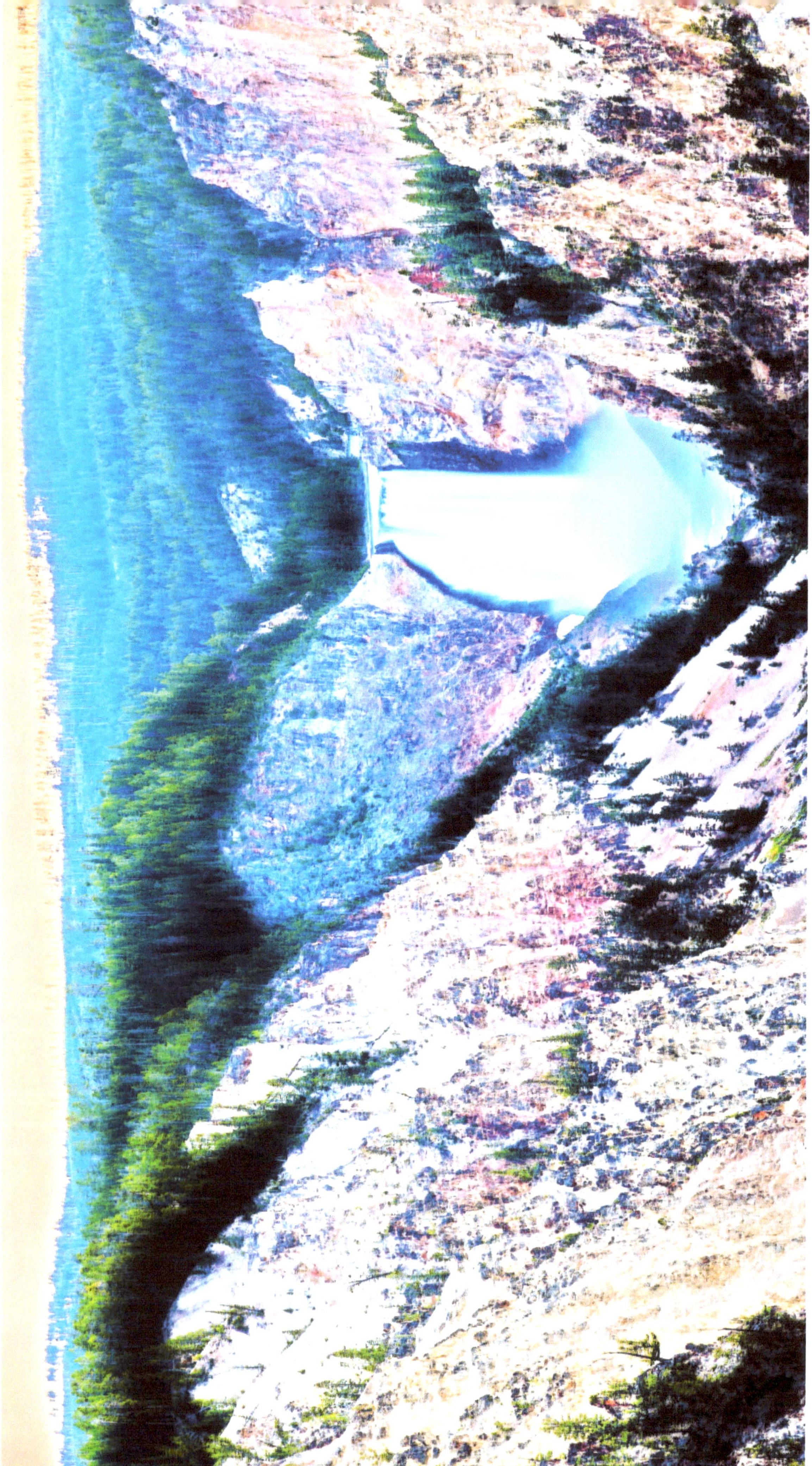

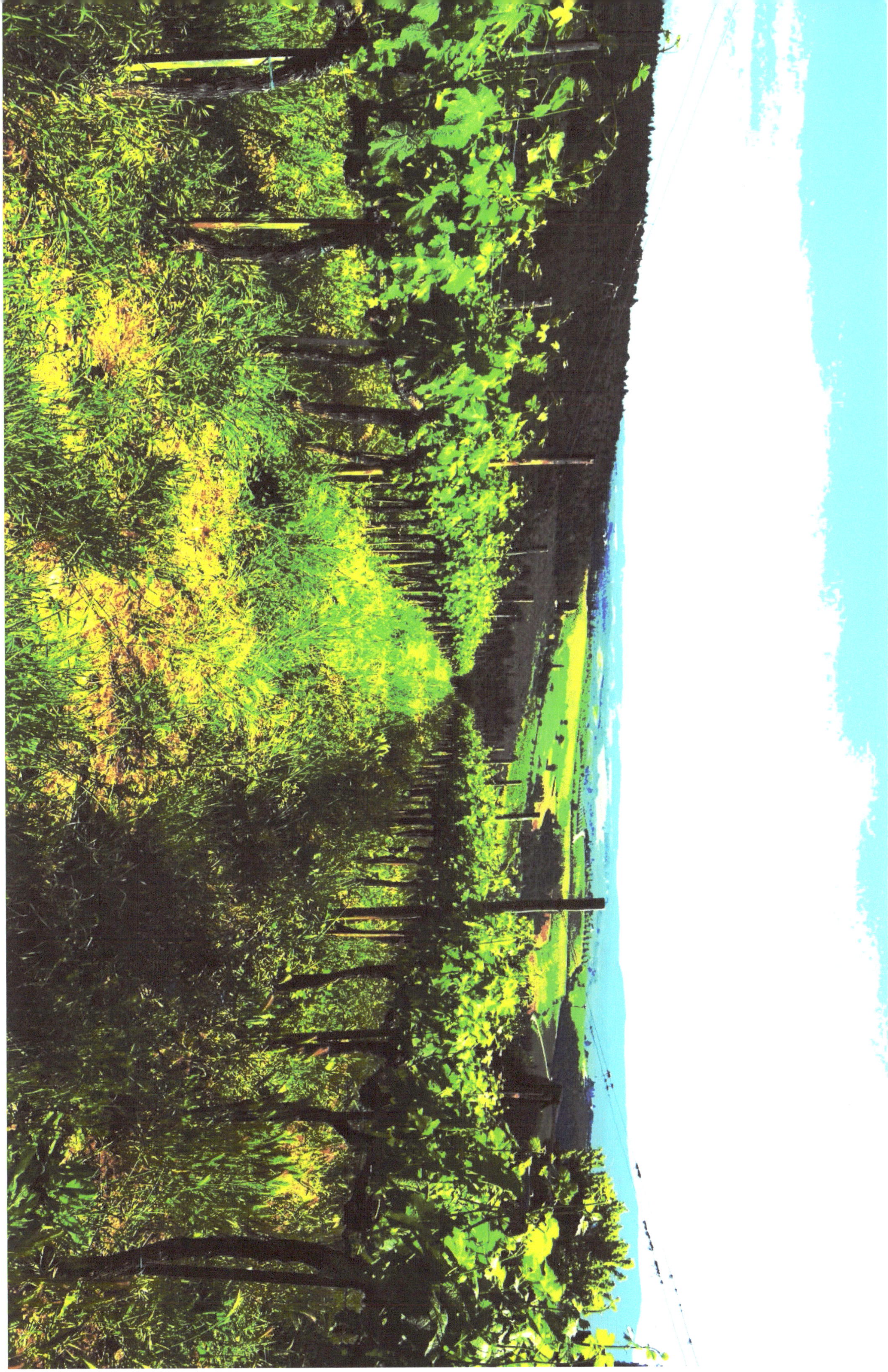

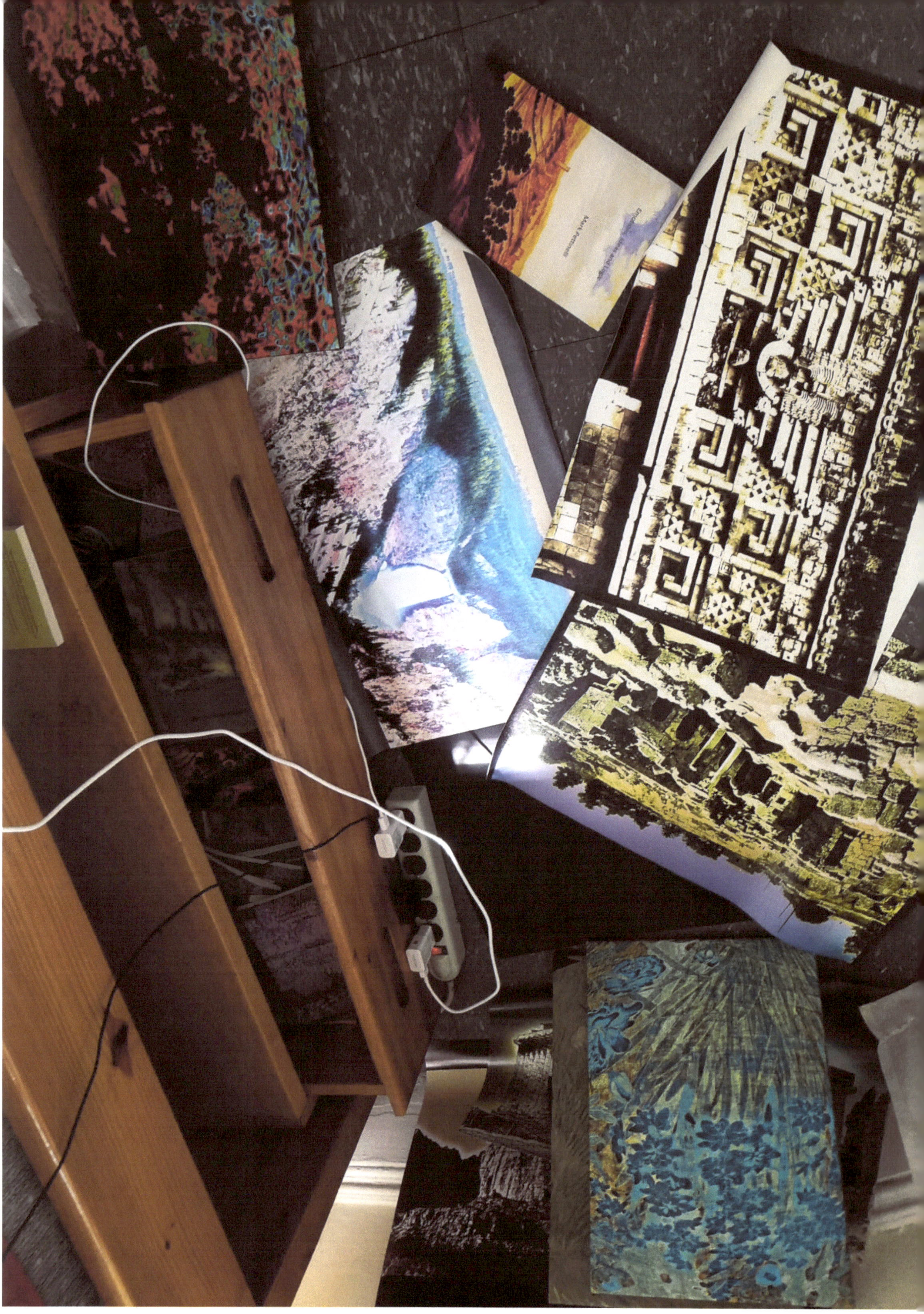
Emotions, Ideas and Logic
Mark Pettinelli

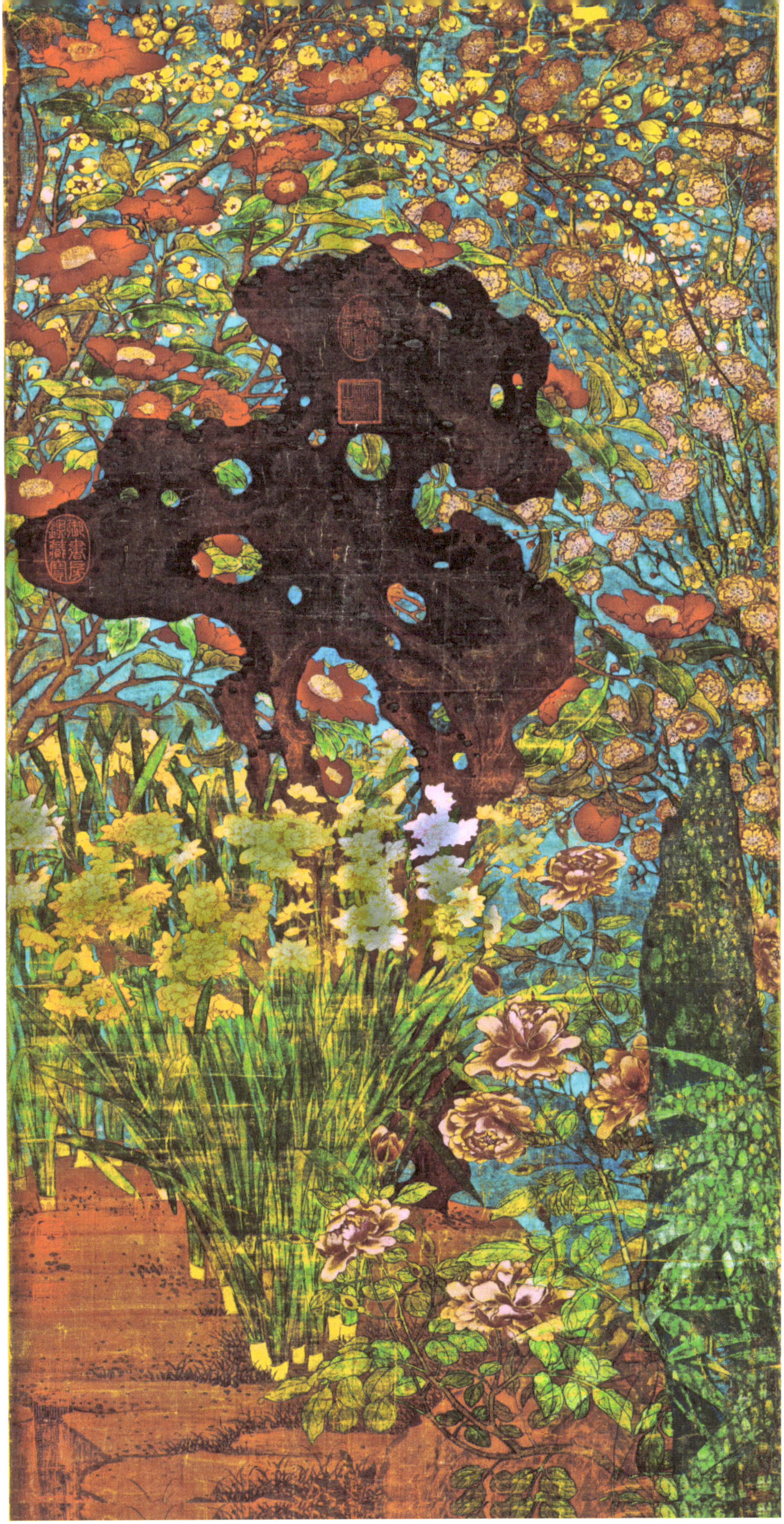

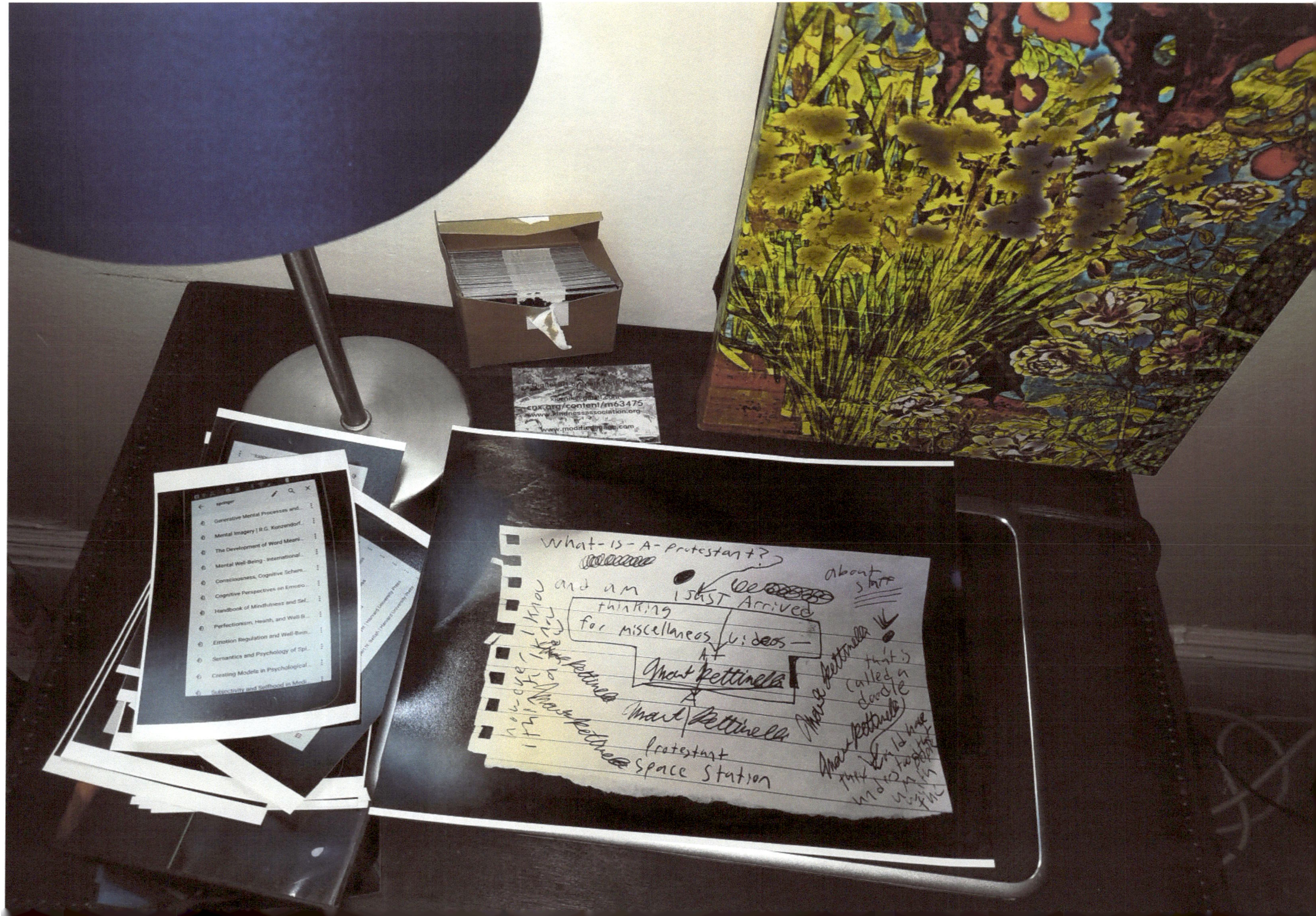

What-is-A-protestant?
and am I just Arrived
thinking
for miscellaneos videos
Mark Kettinella
Mark Kettinella
protestant
Space Station
about stuff
that is called a doodle

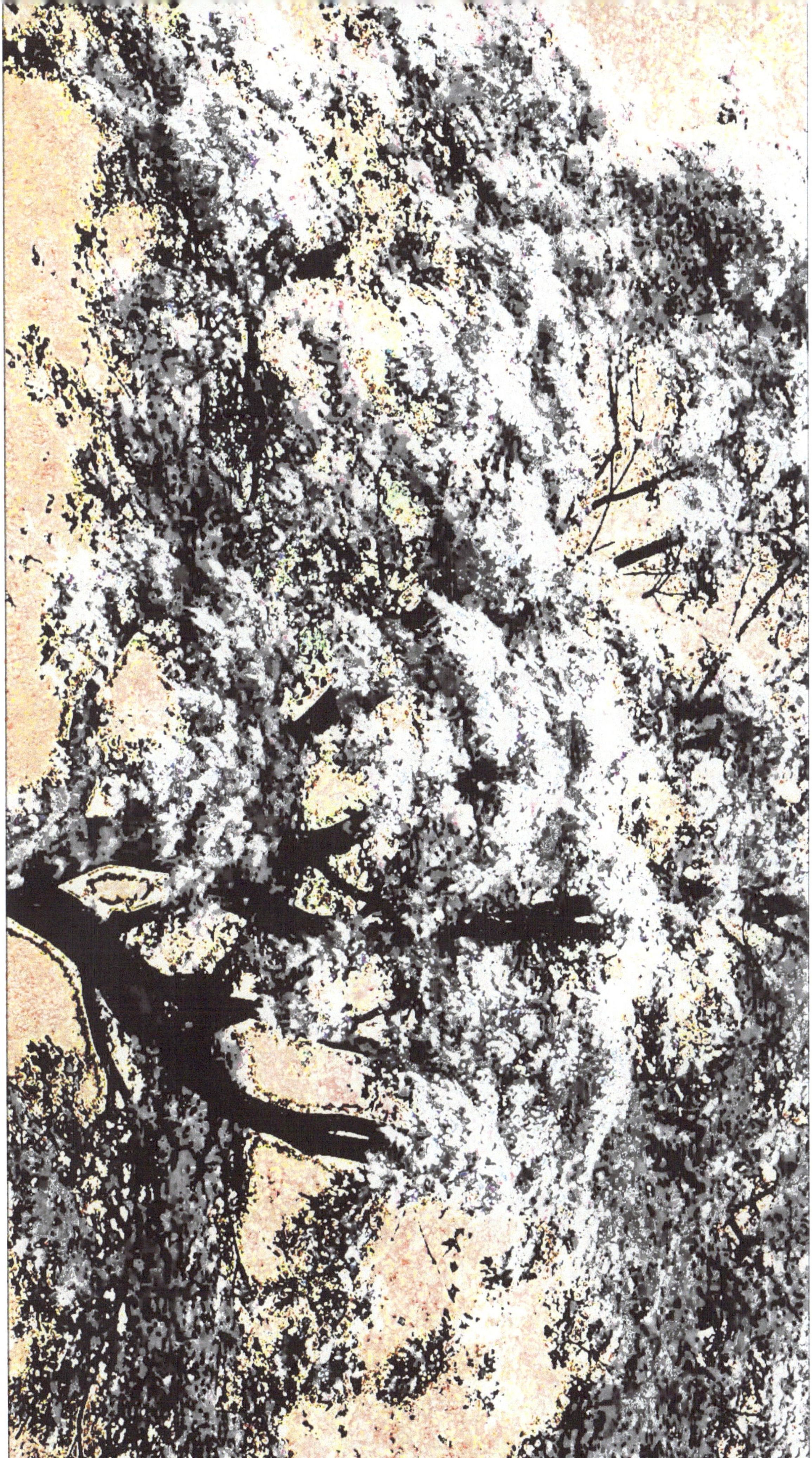

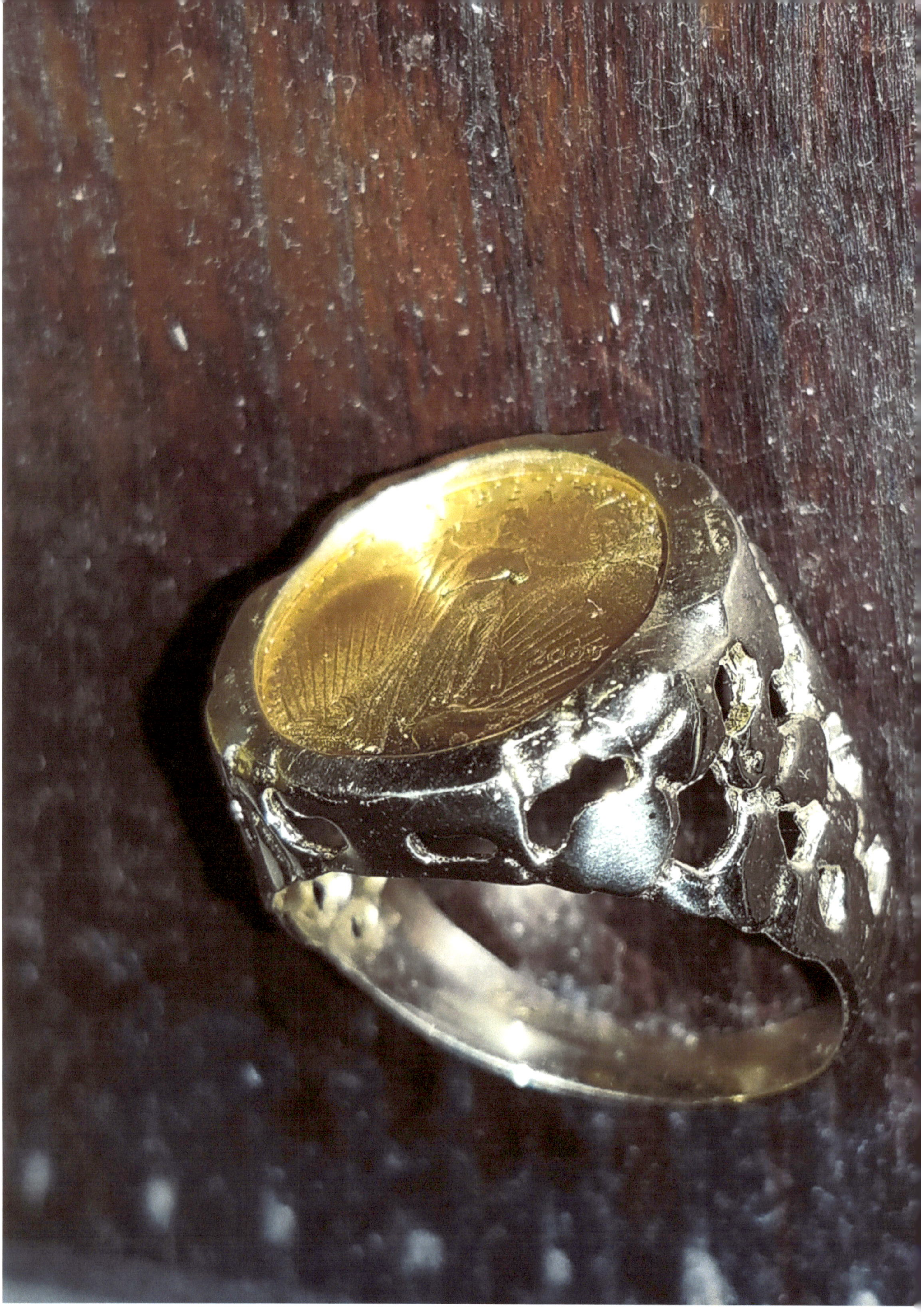

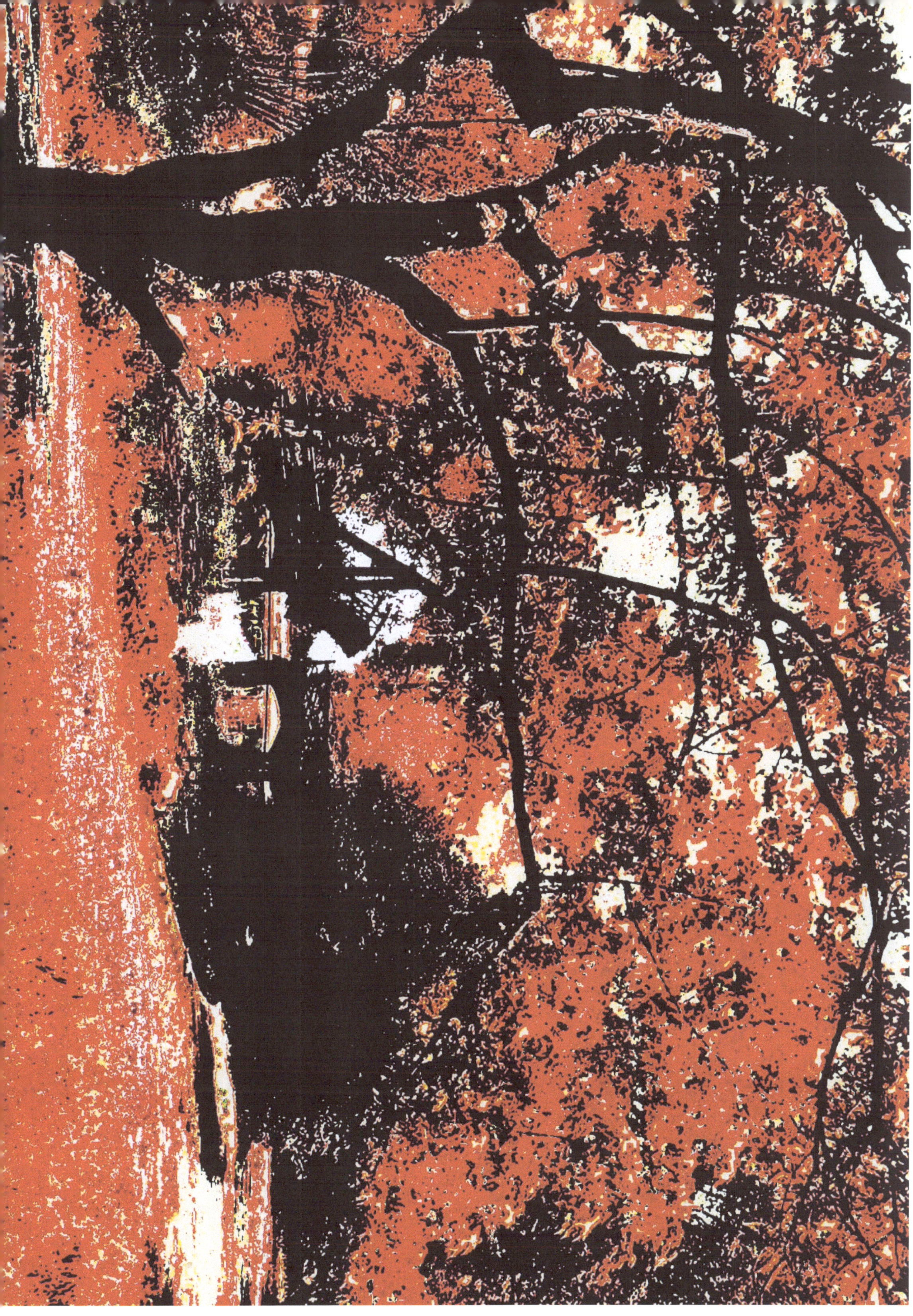

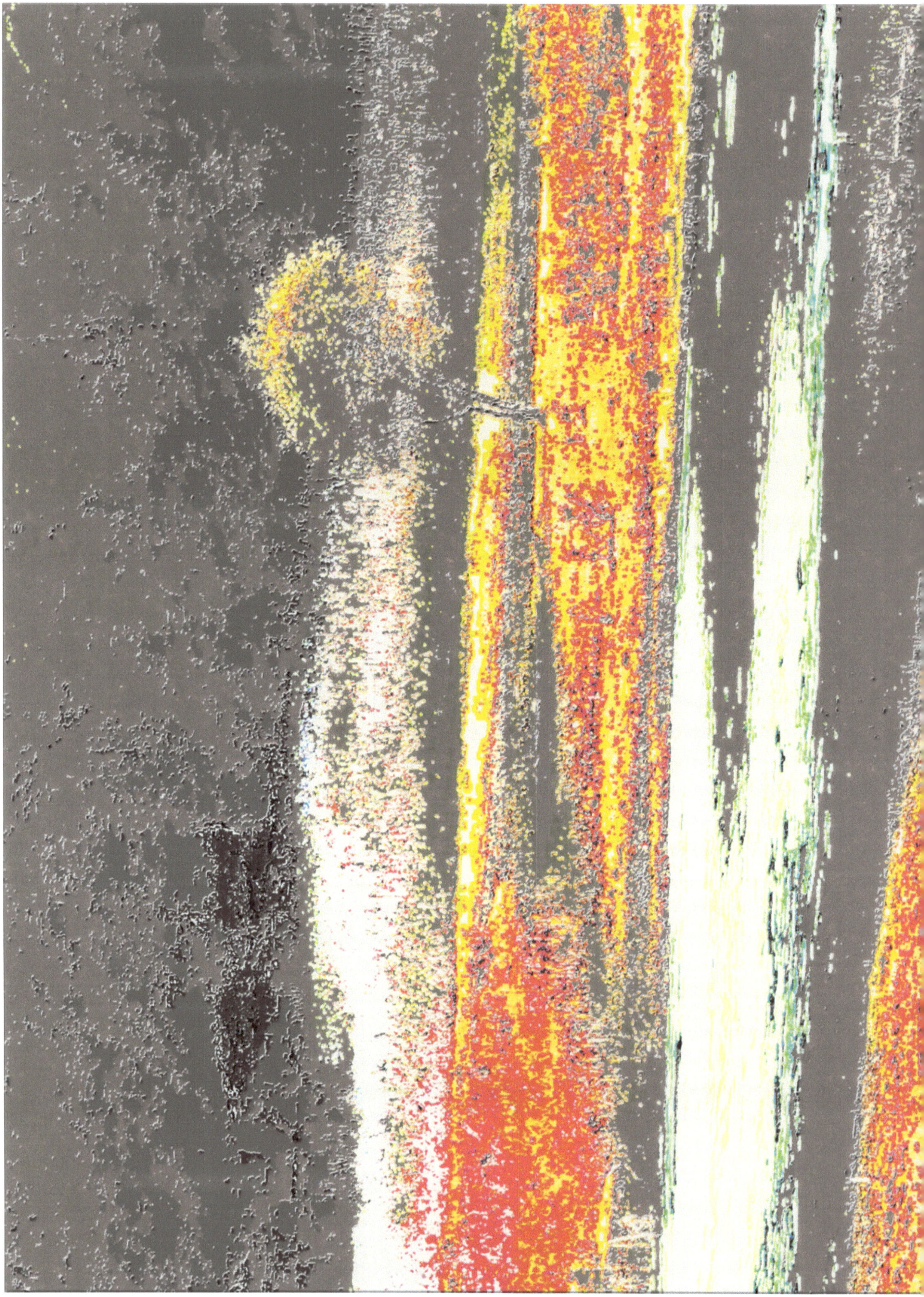

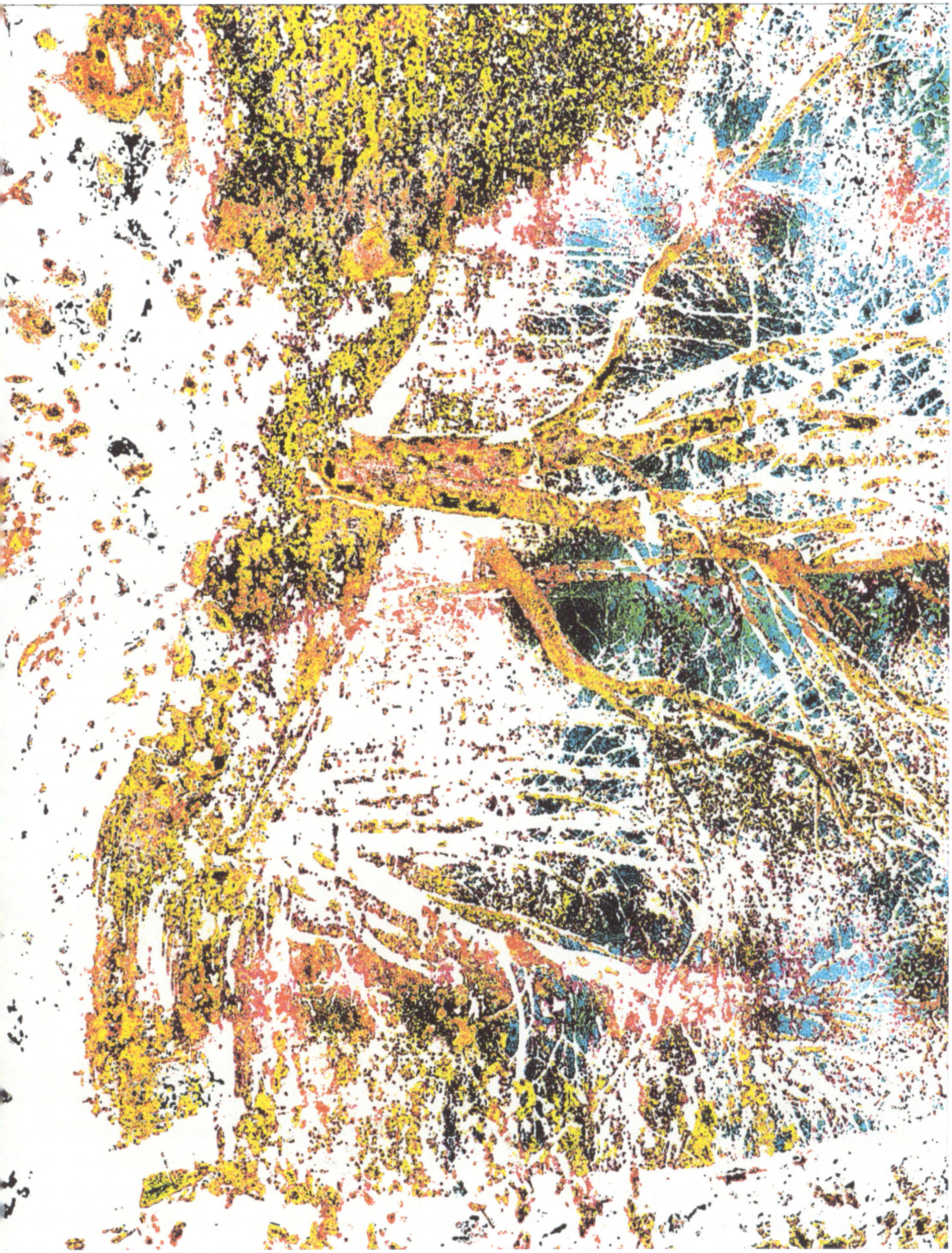

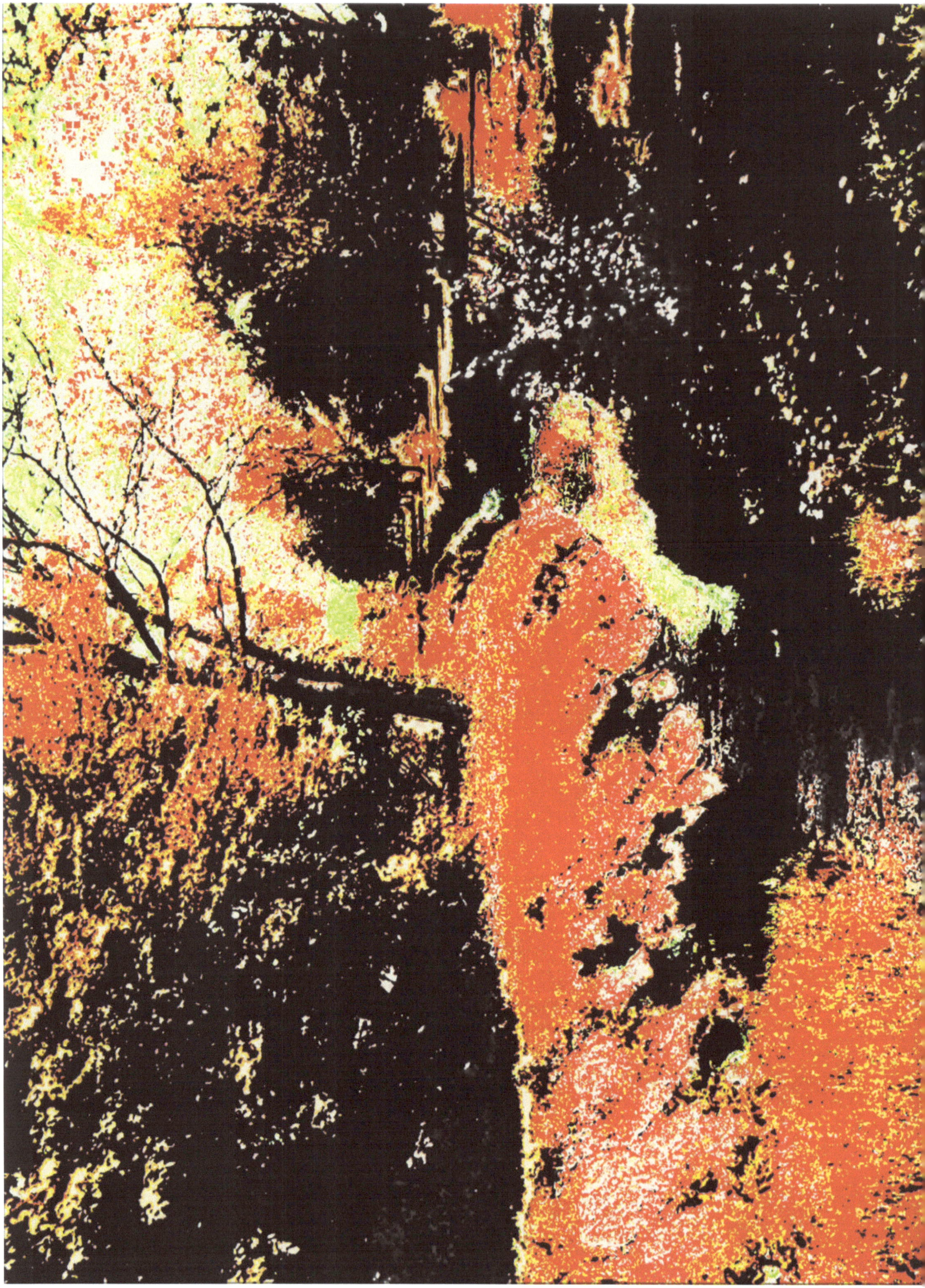

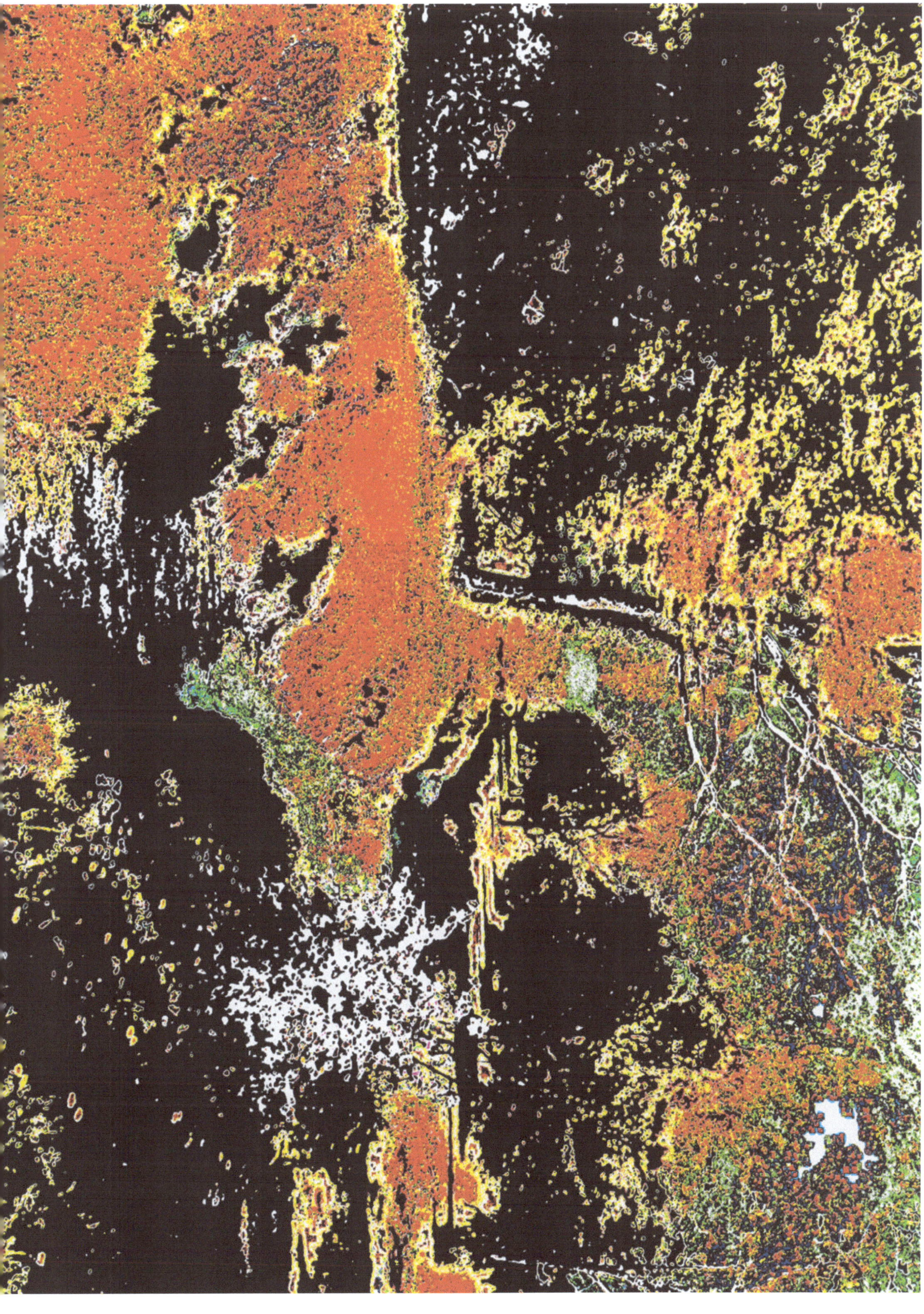

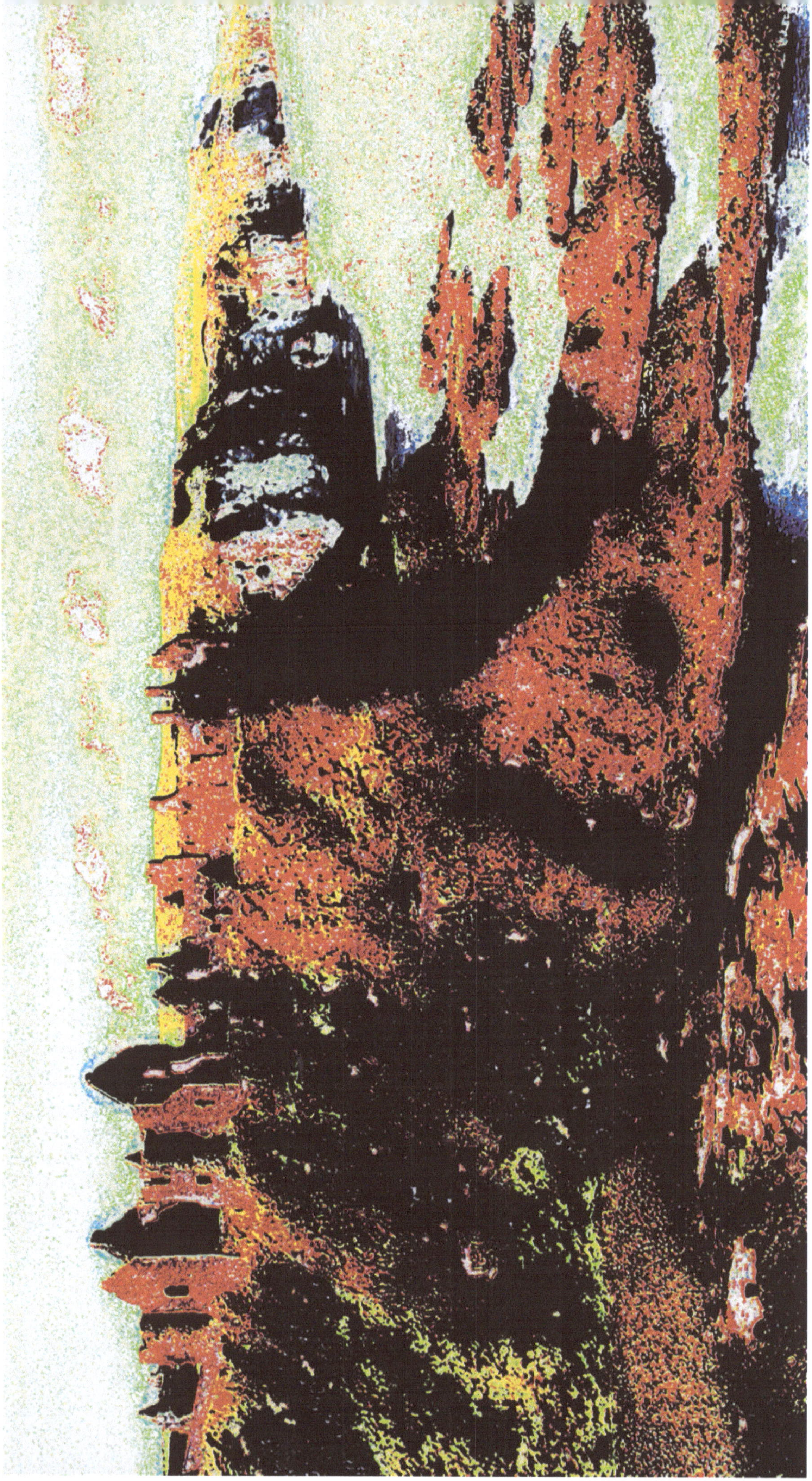

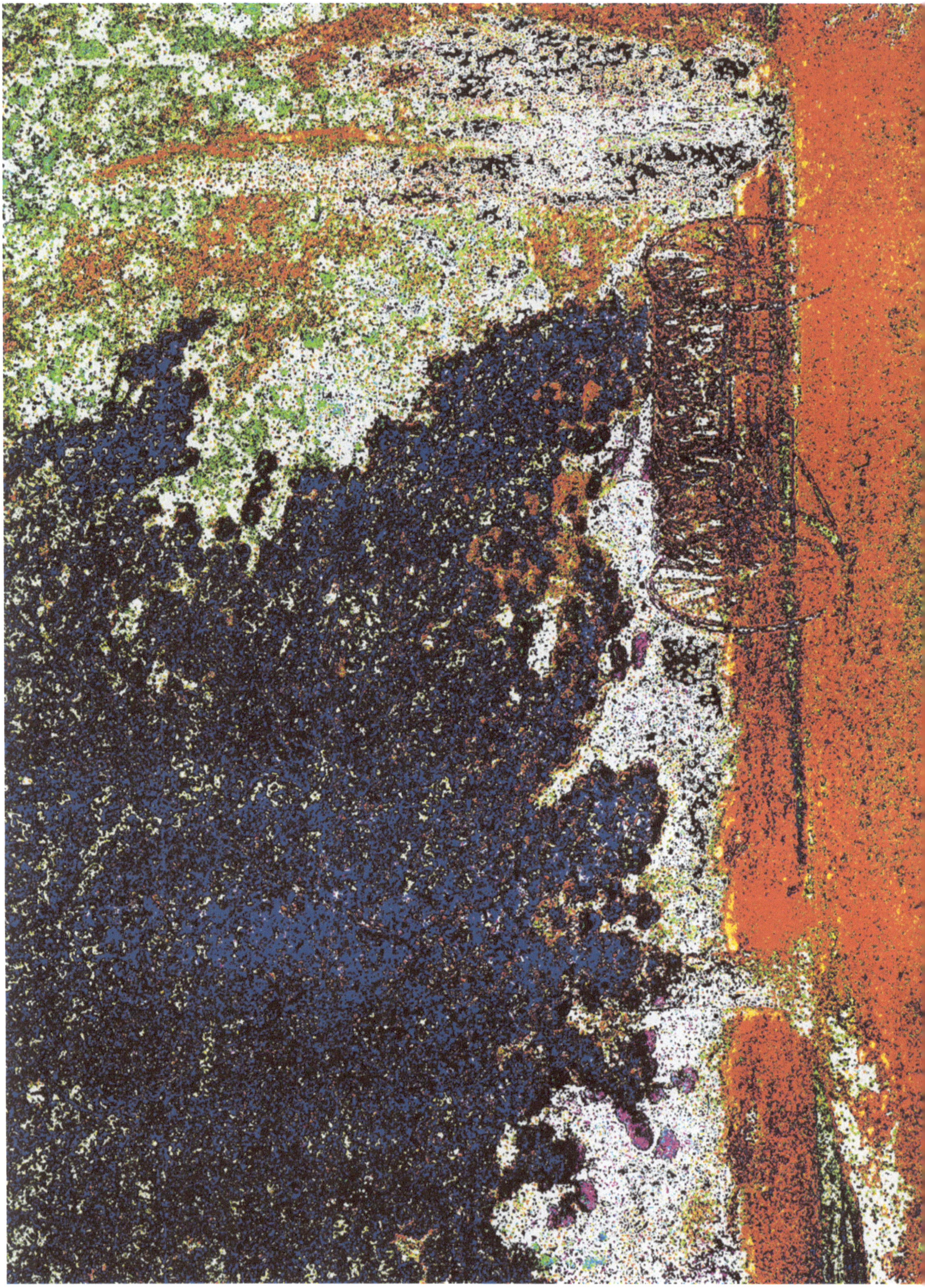

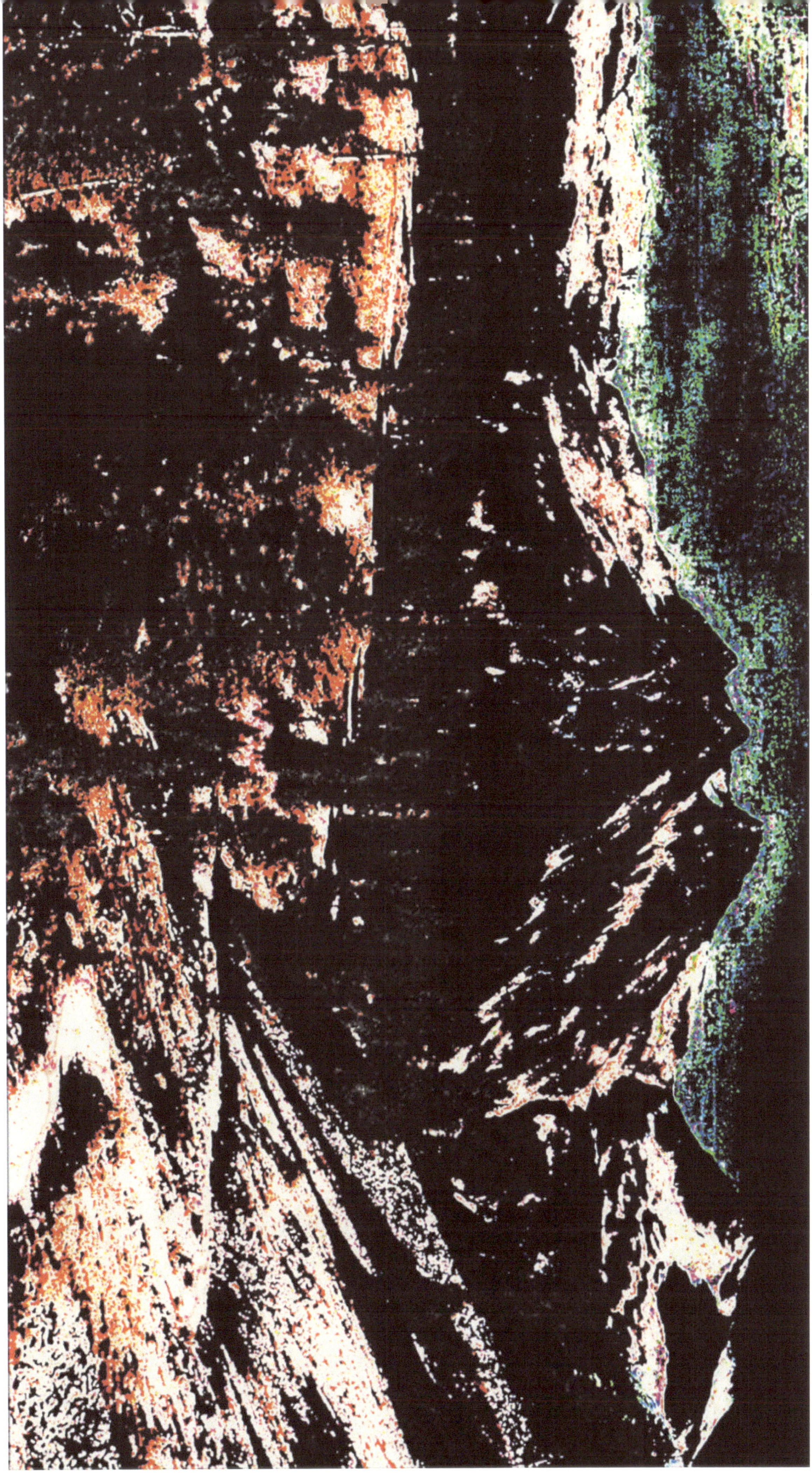

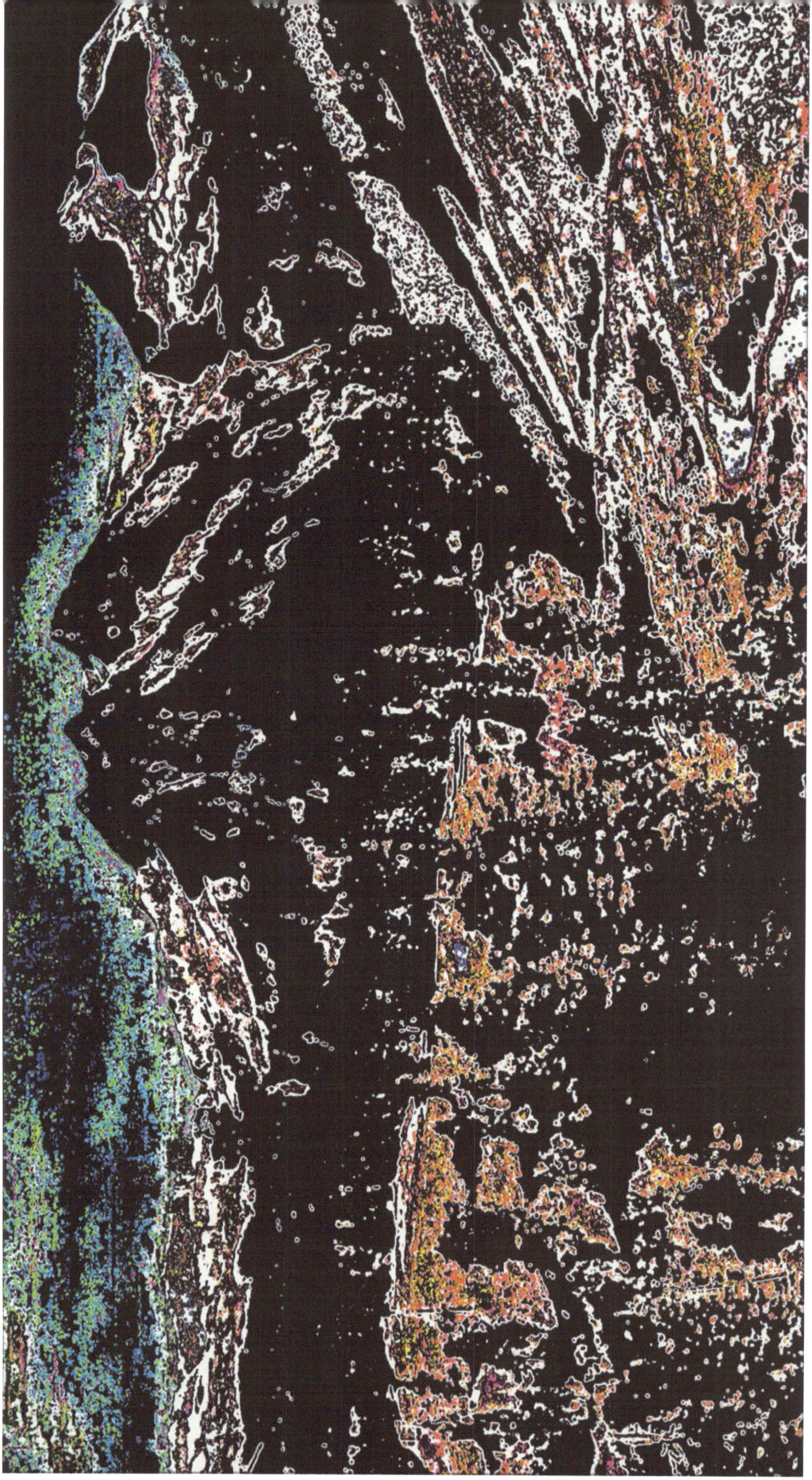

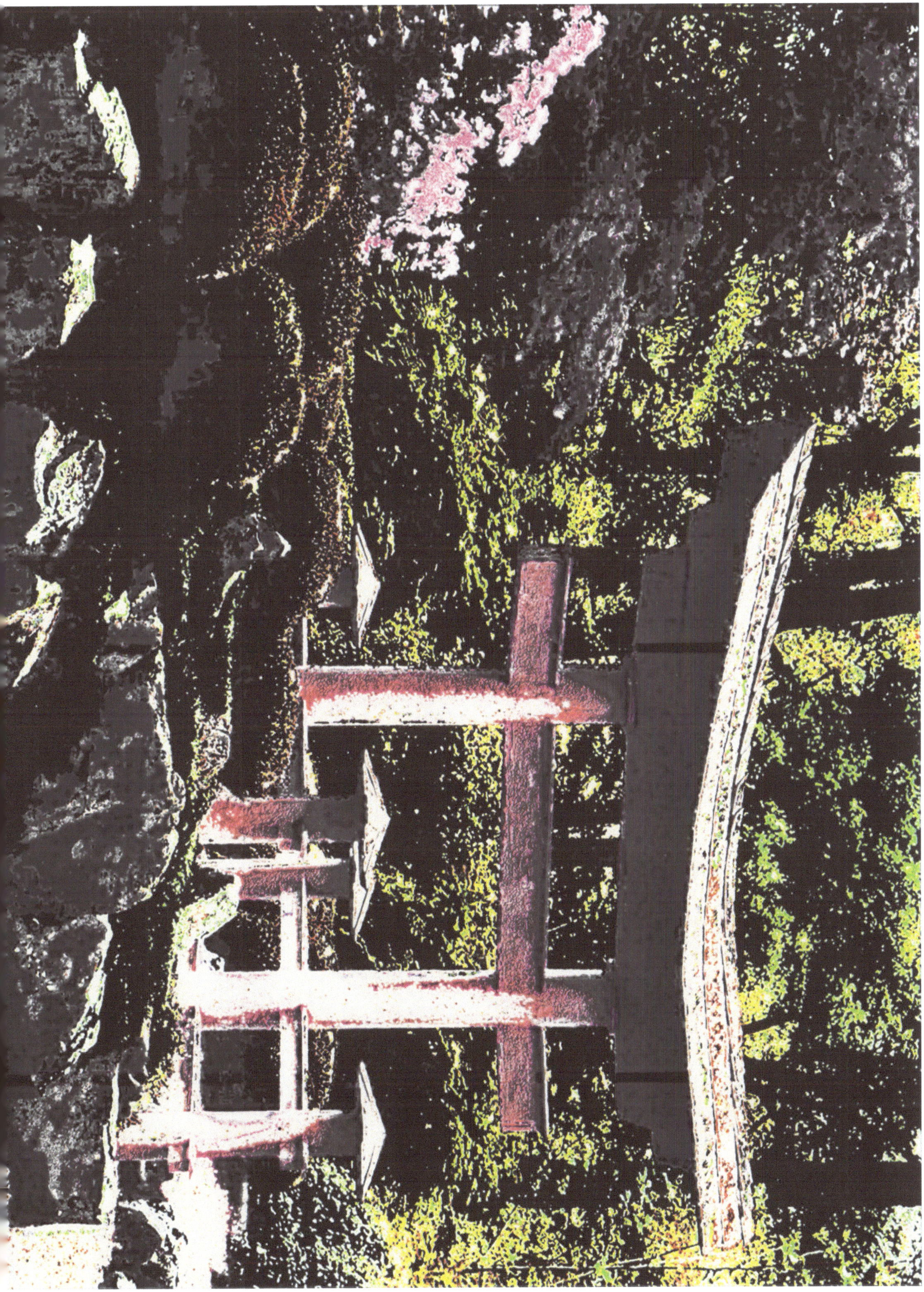

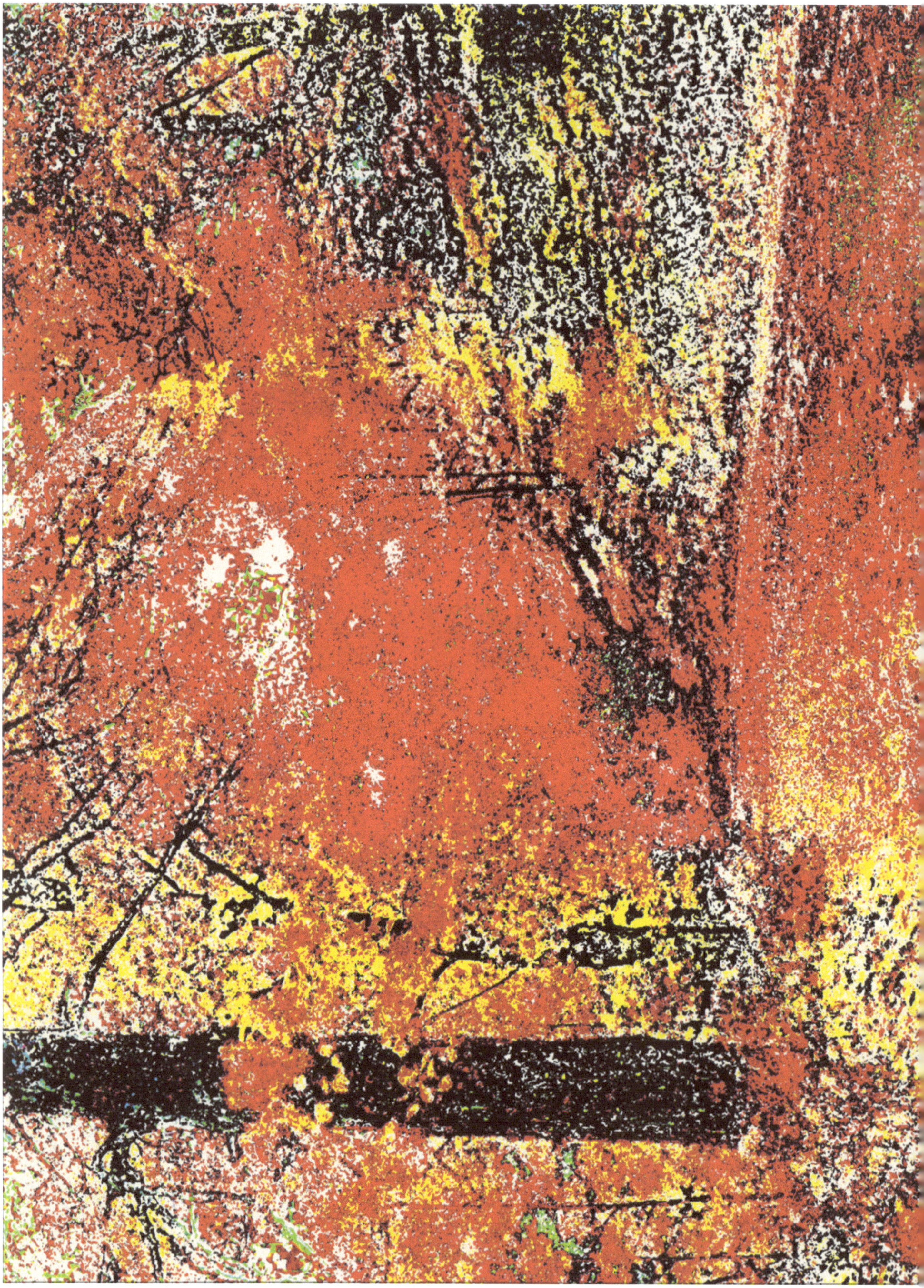

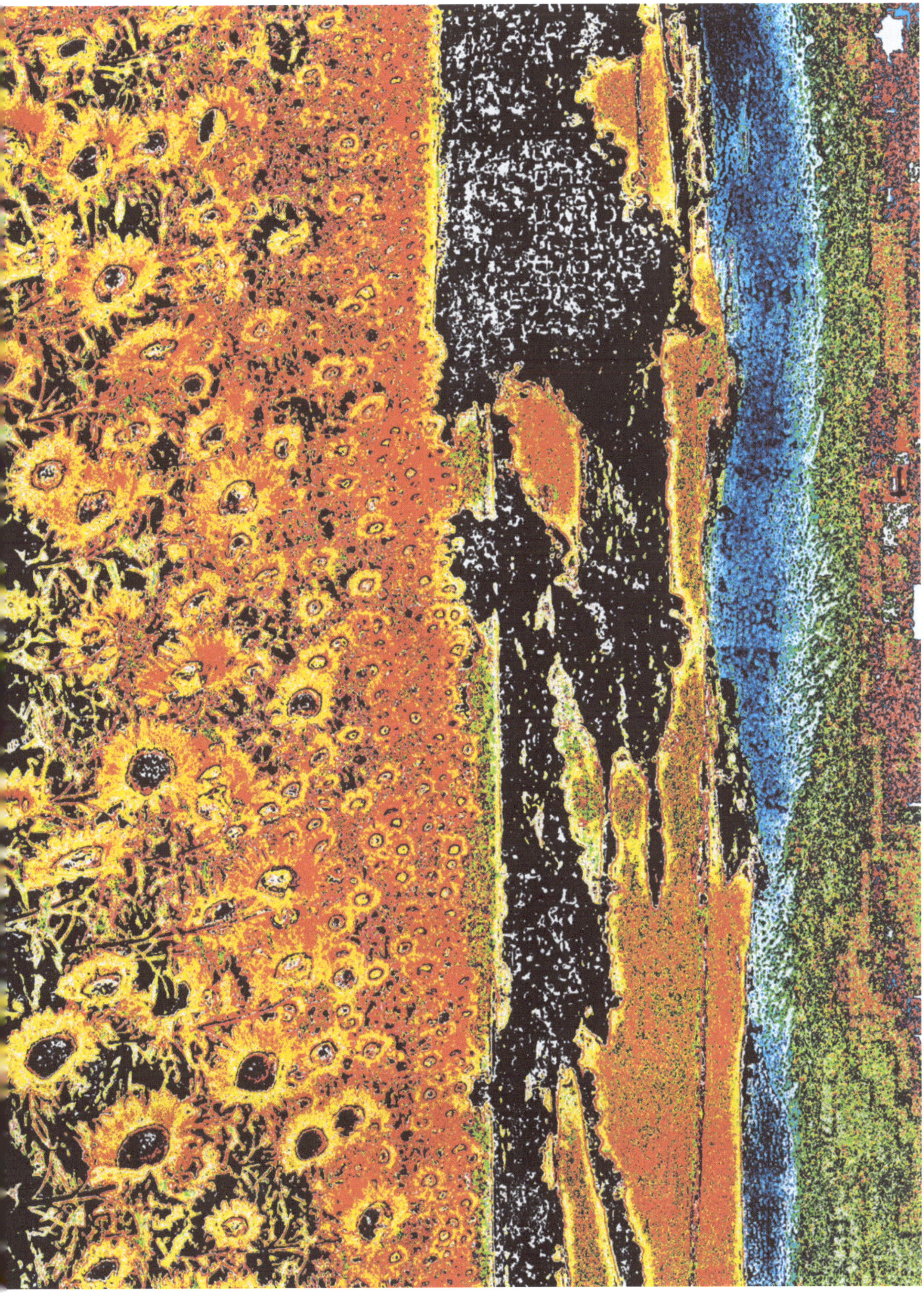

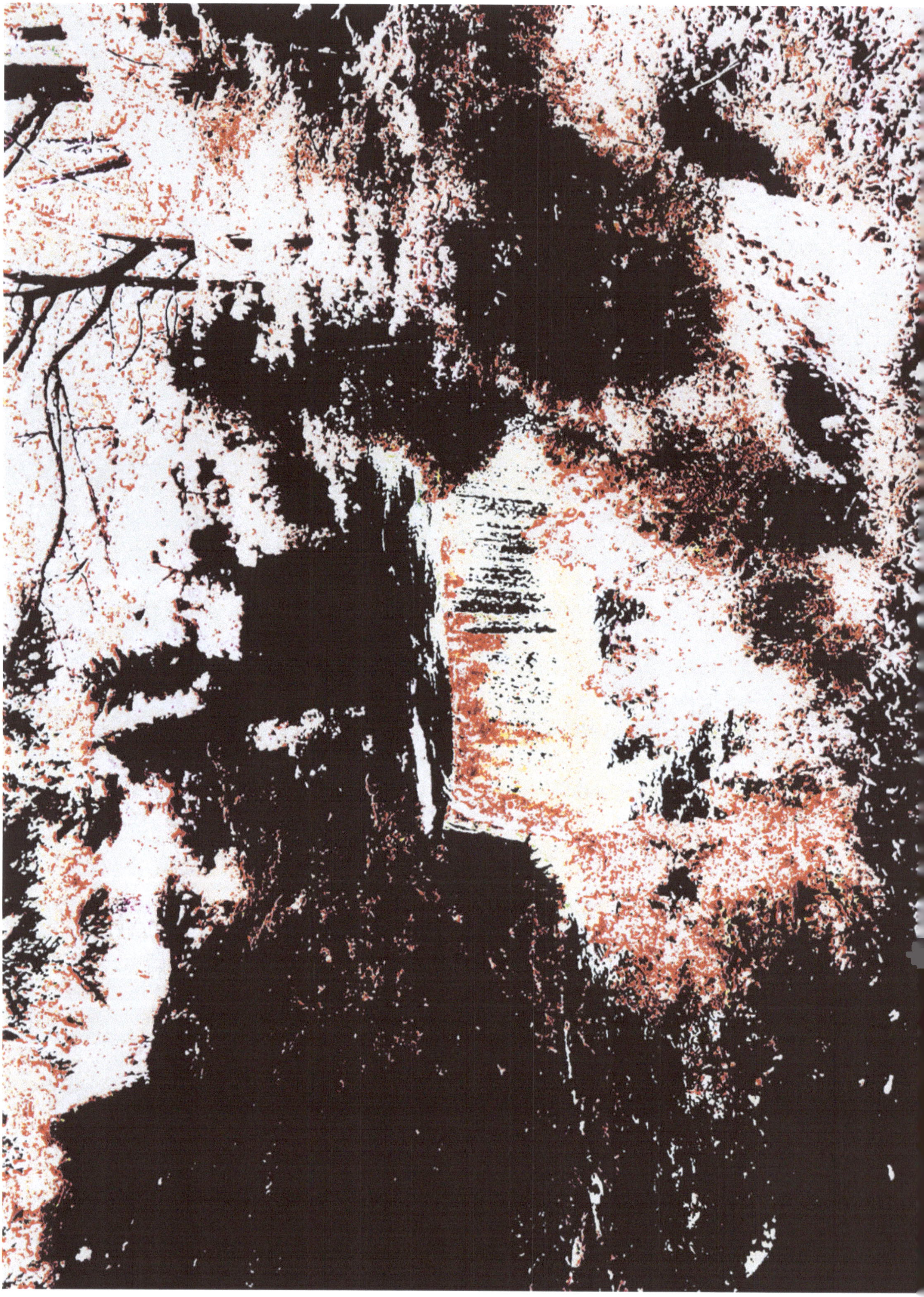

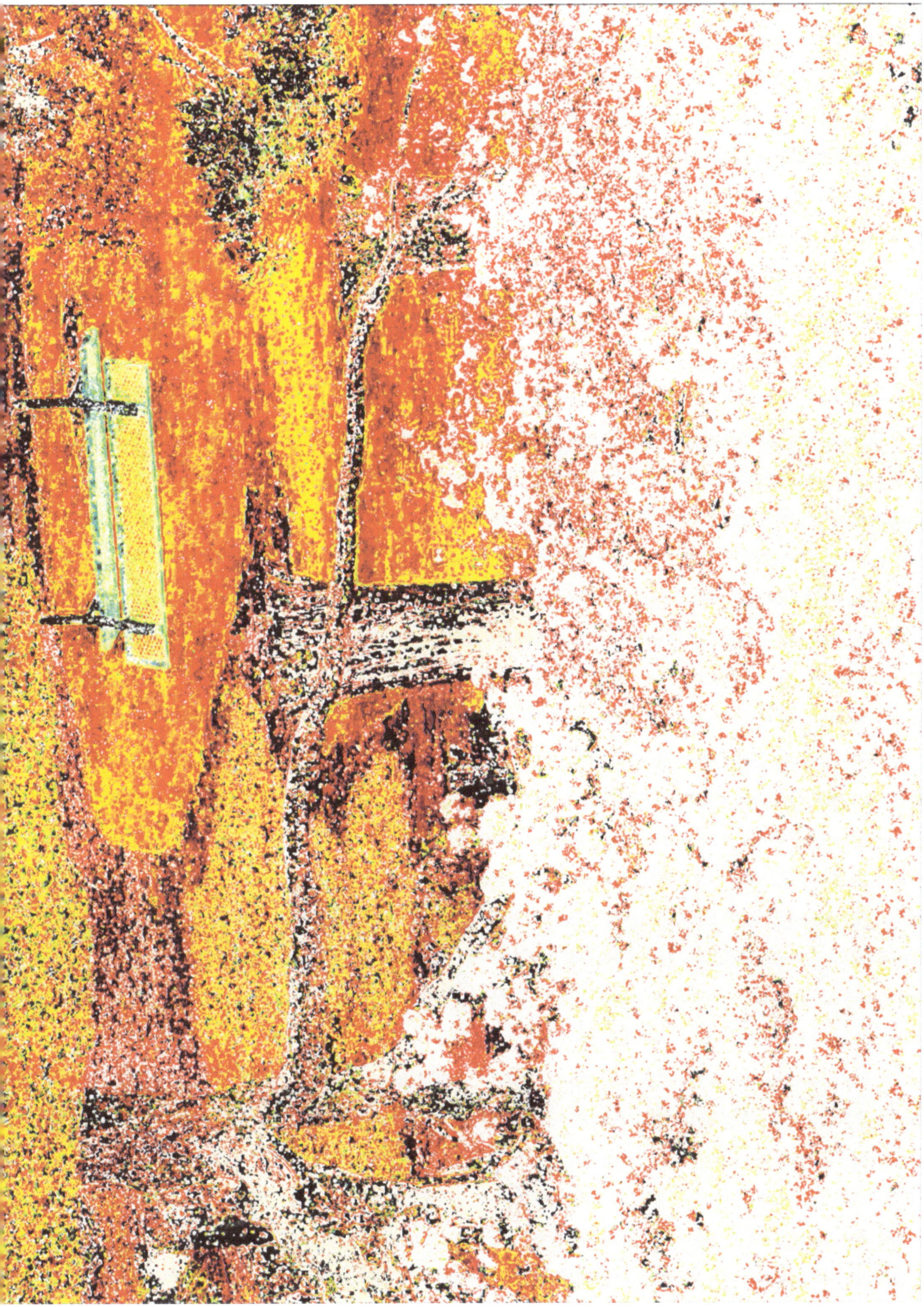

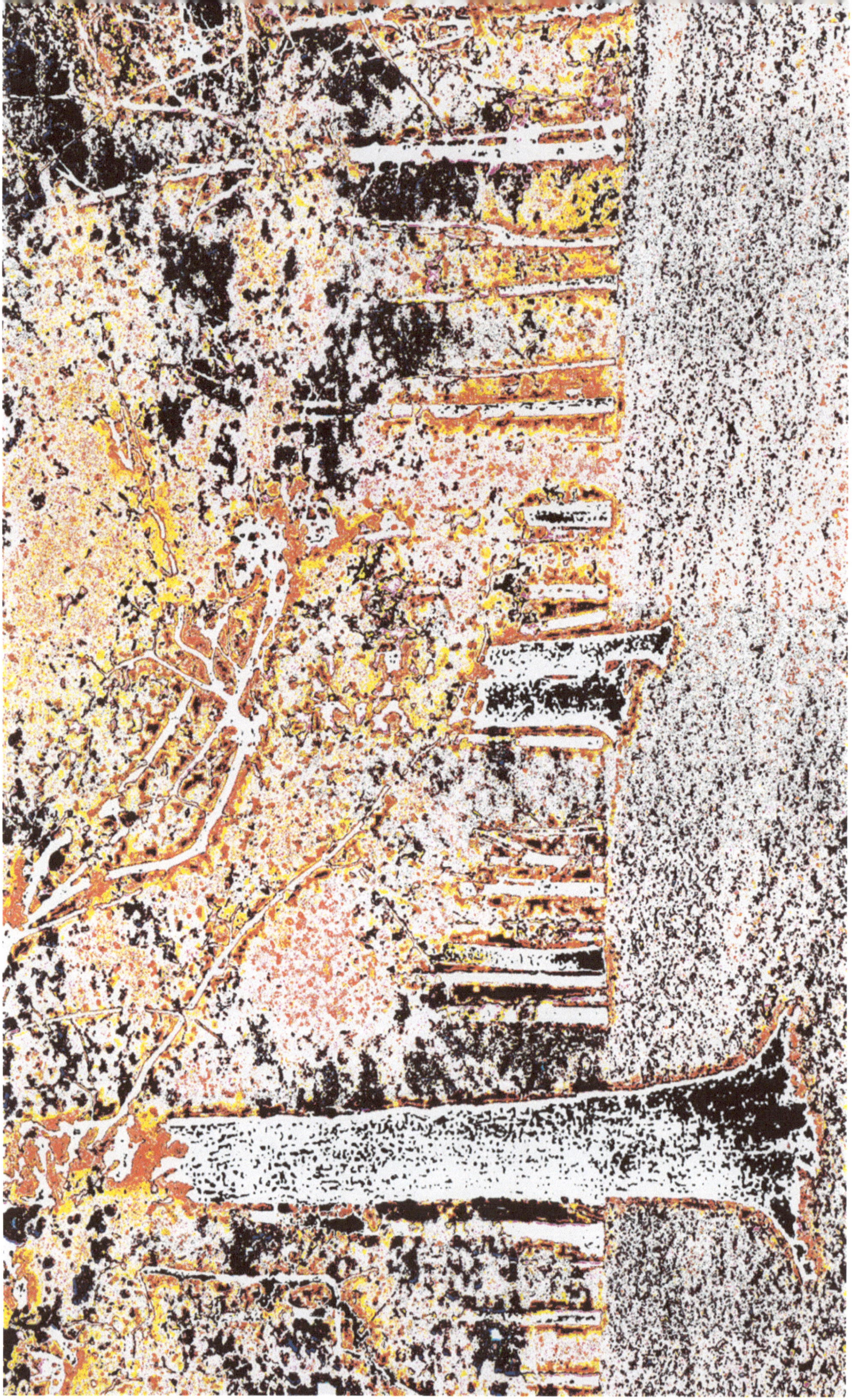

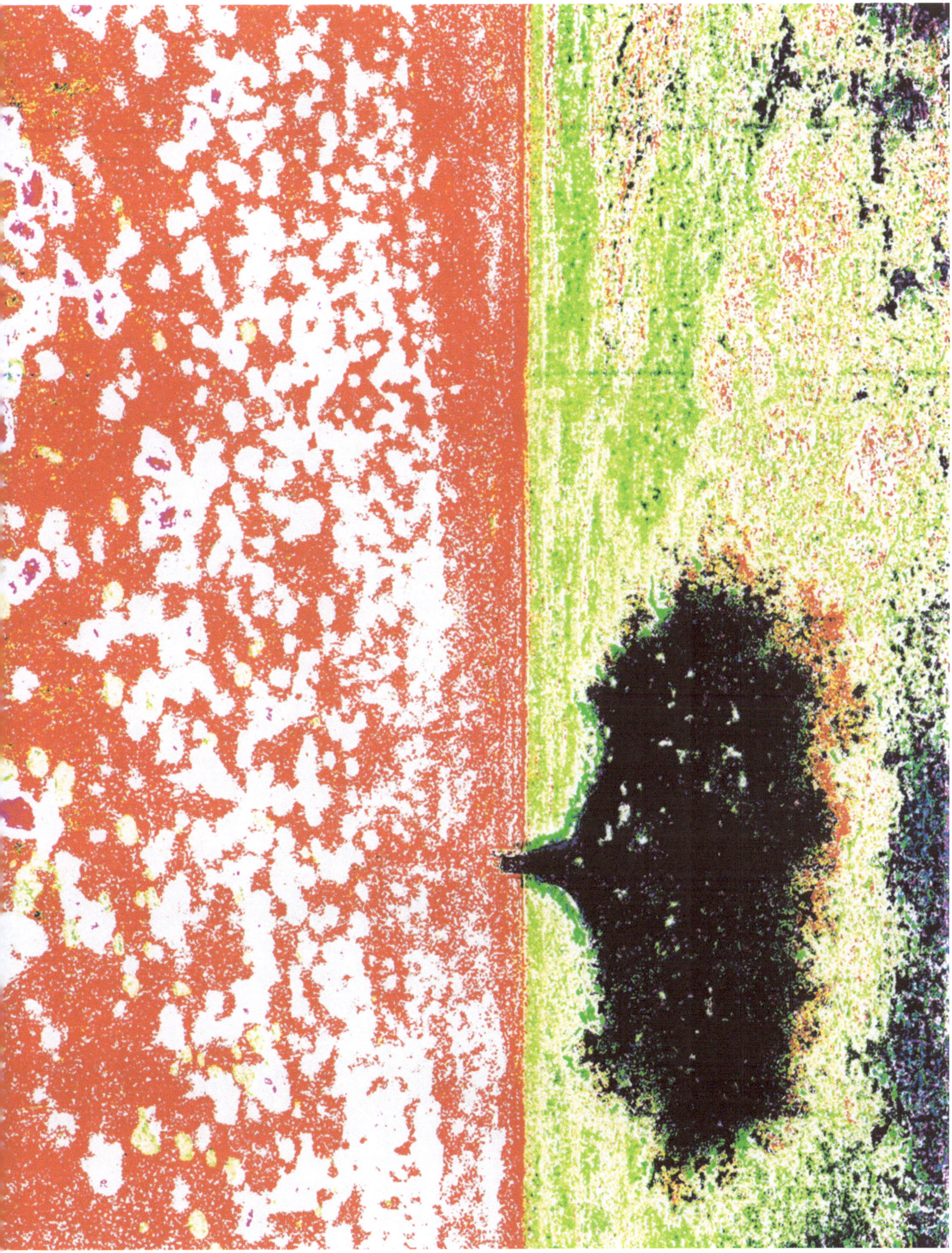

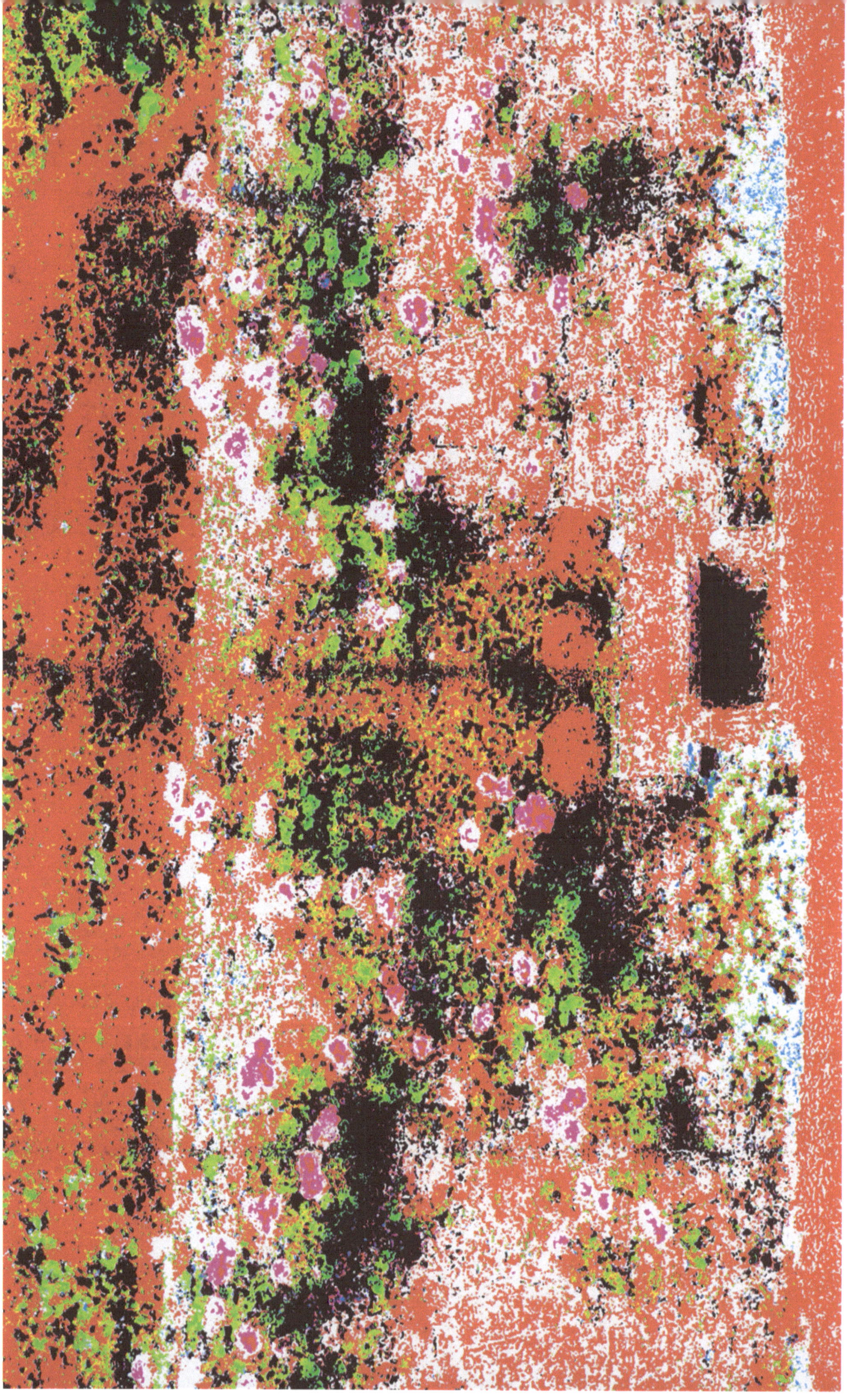

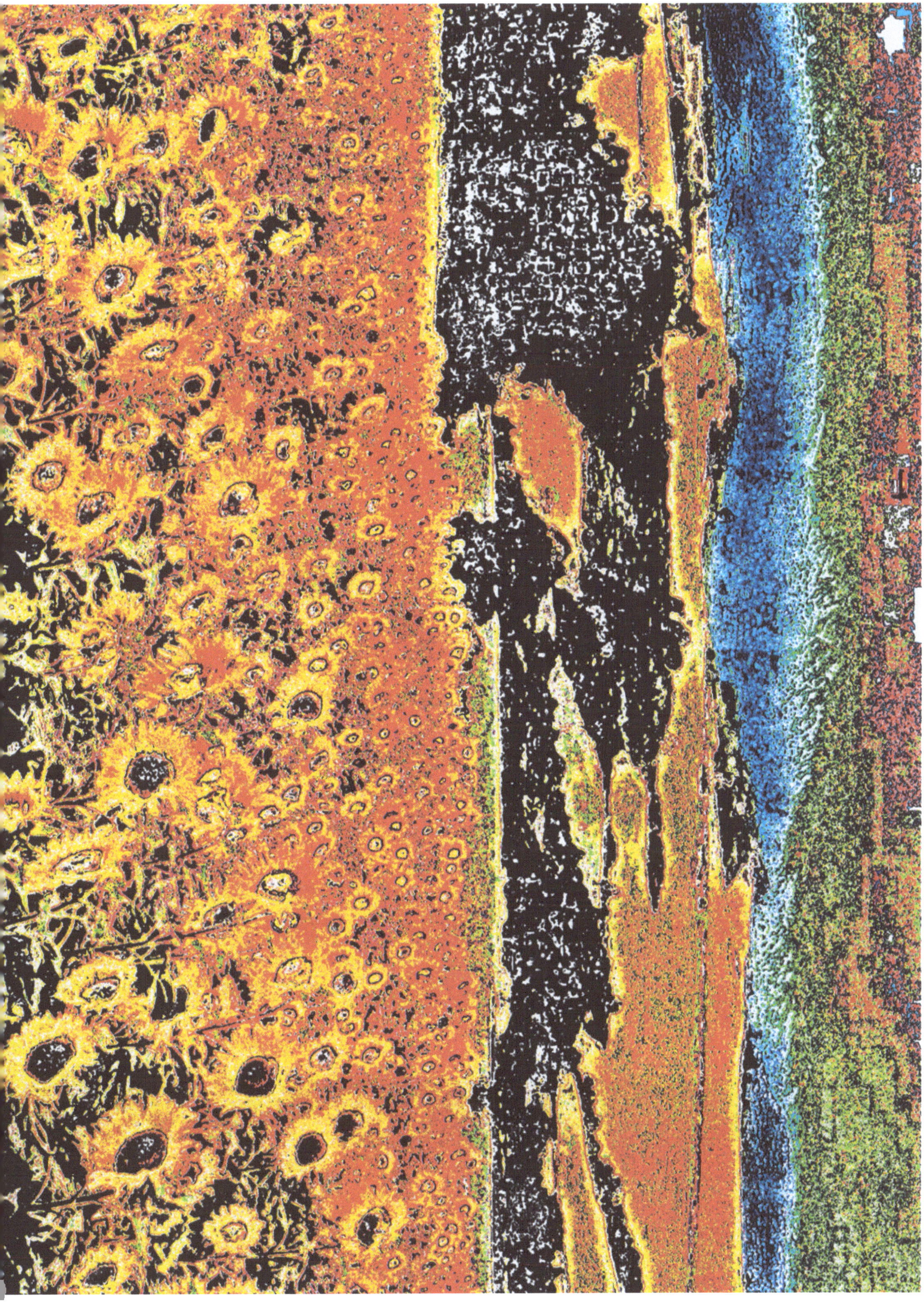

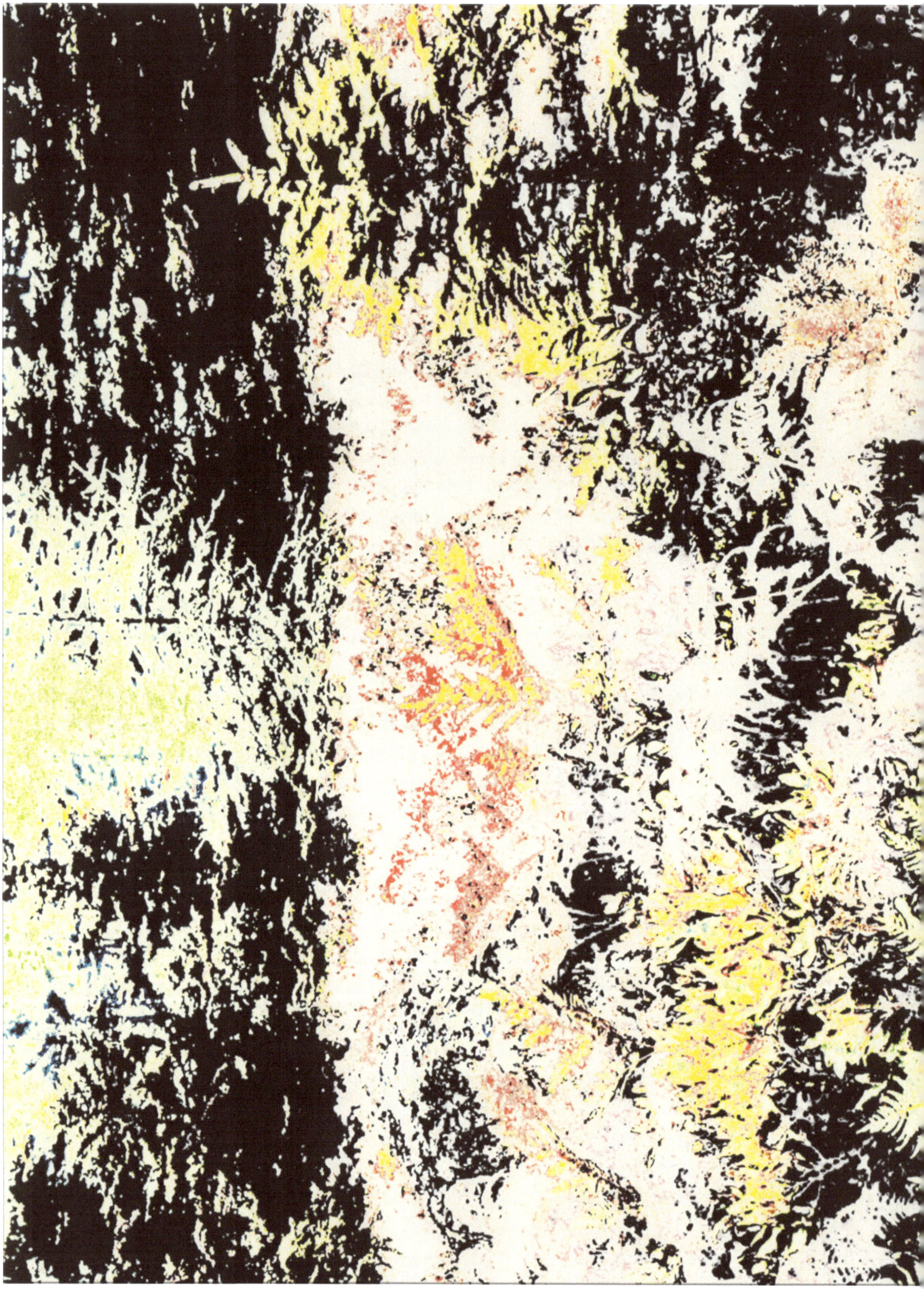

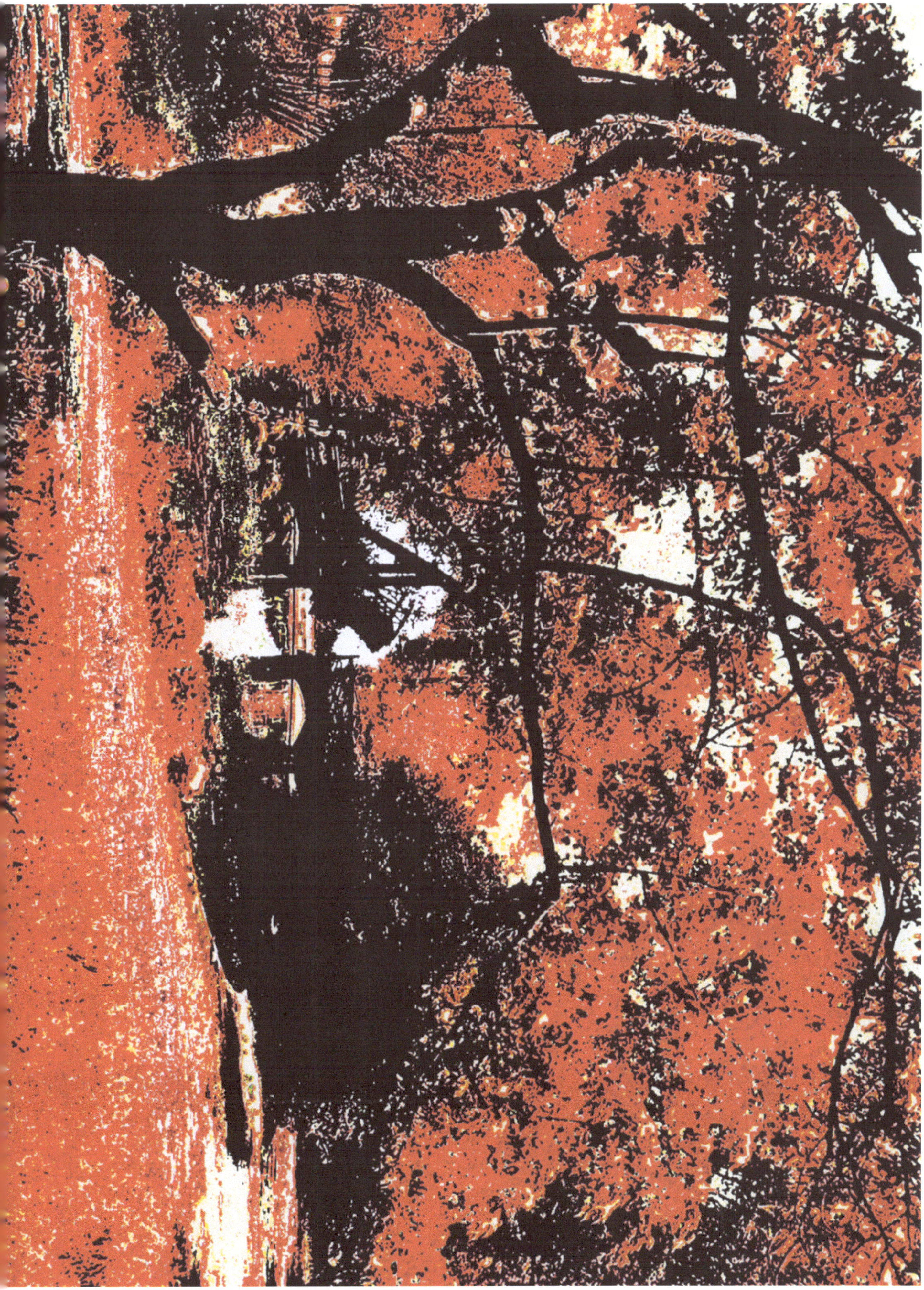

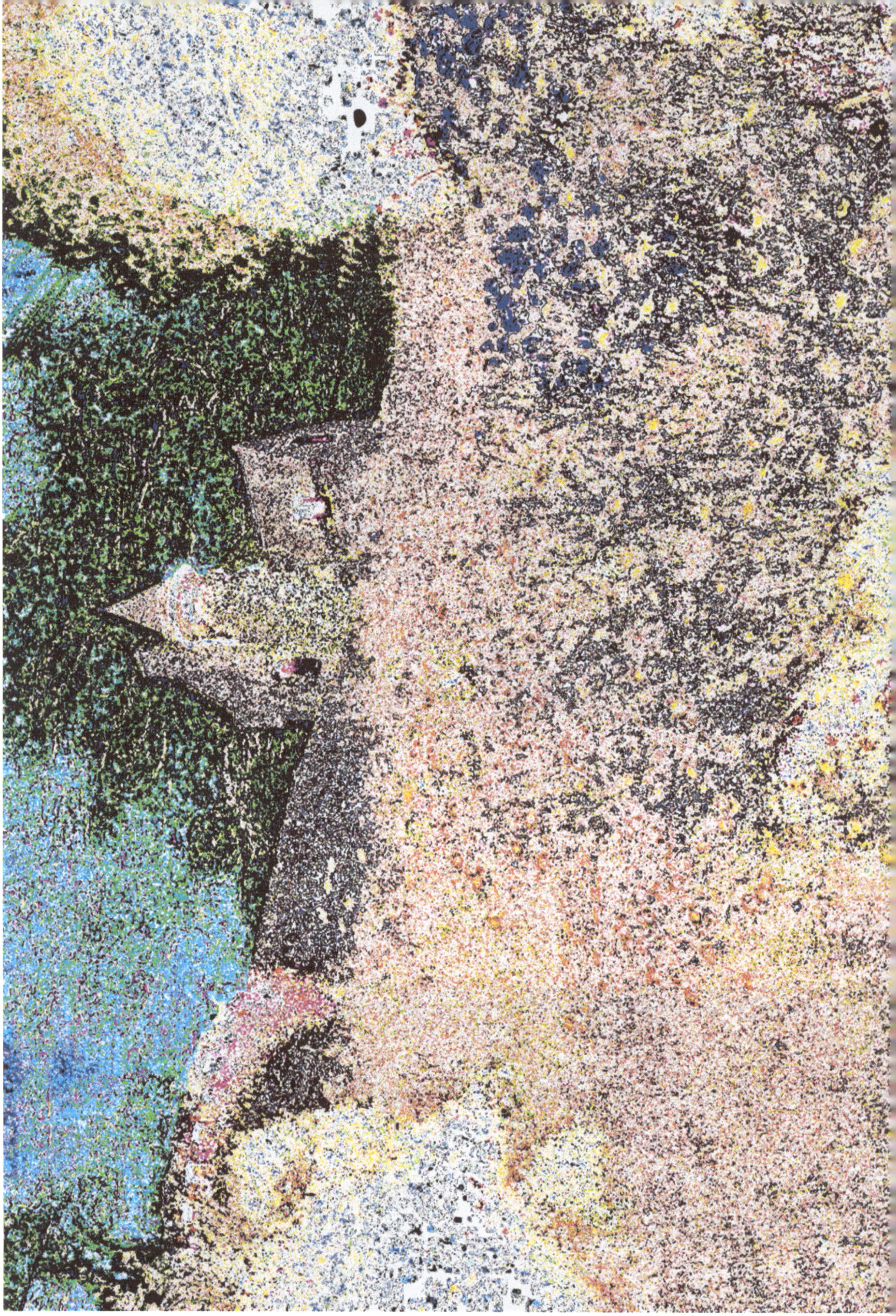

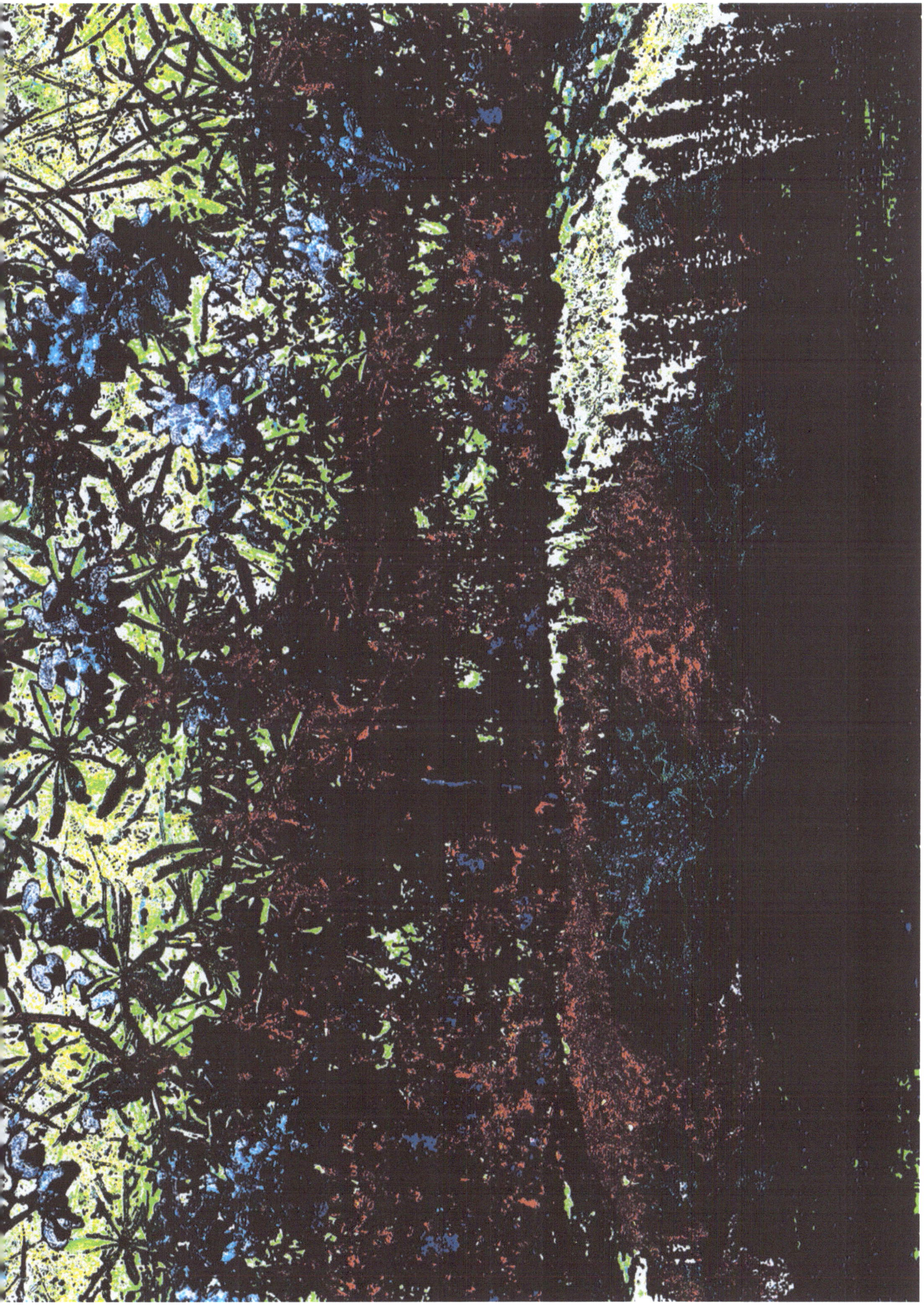

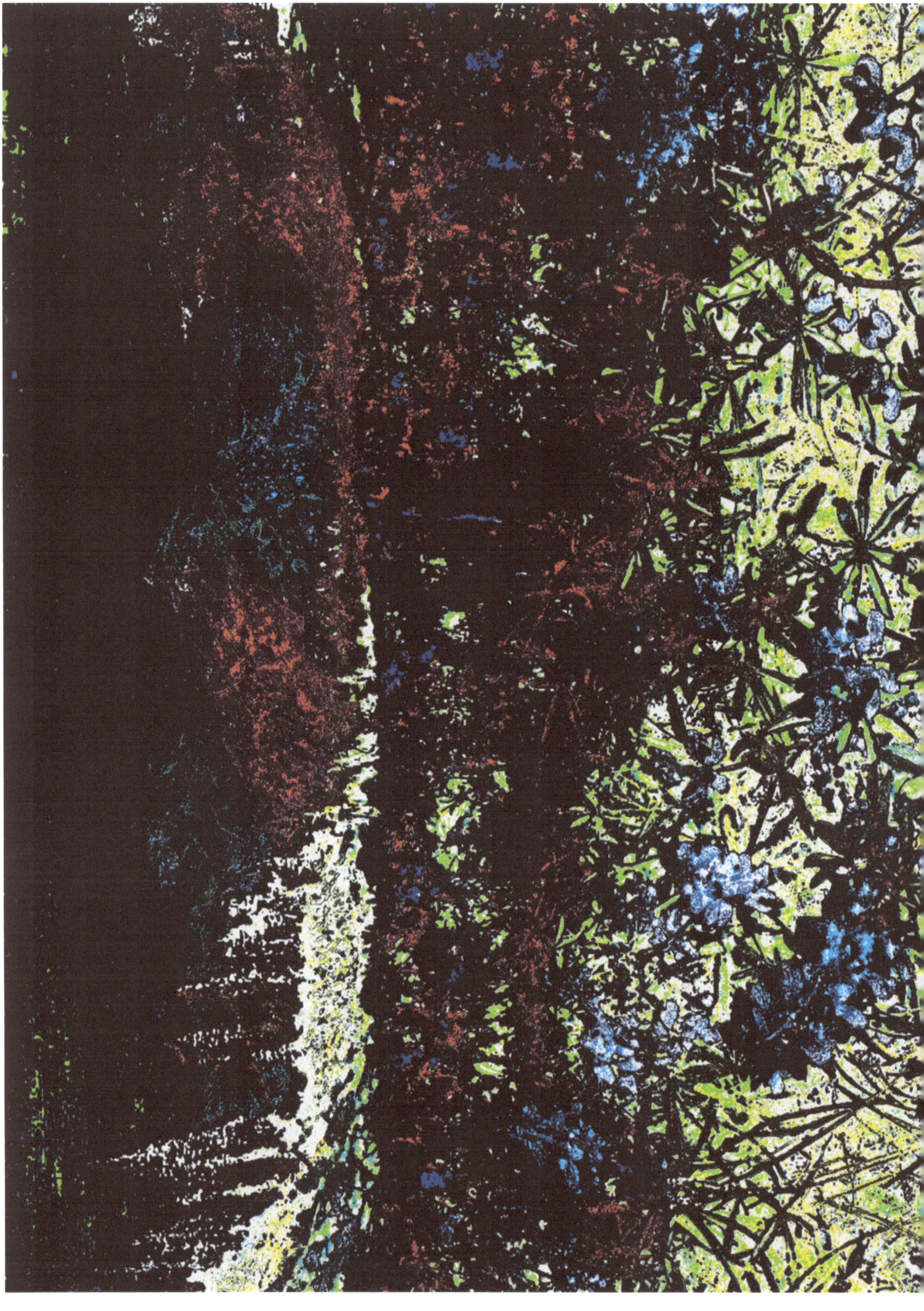

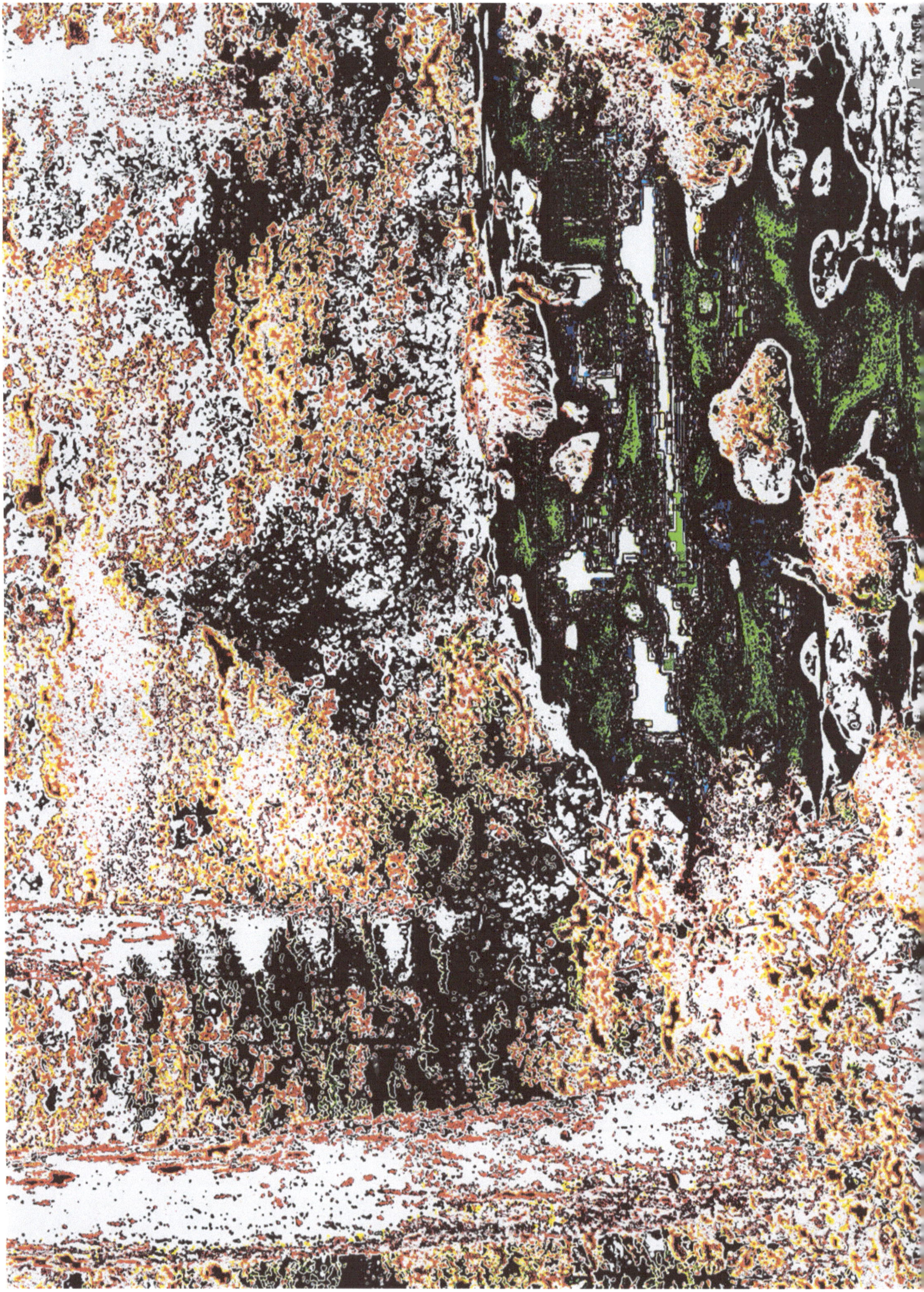

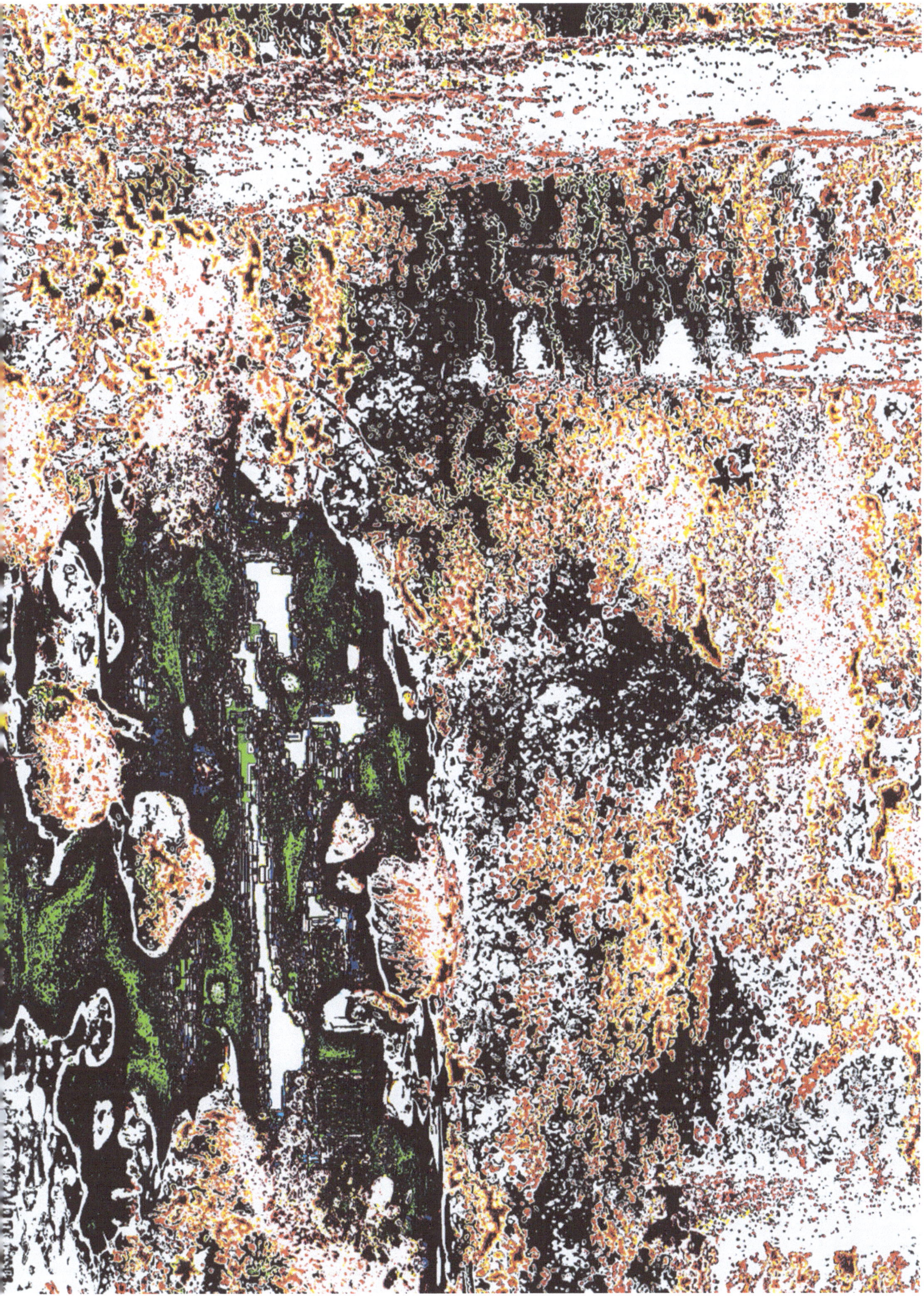

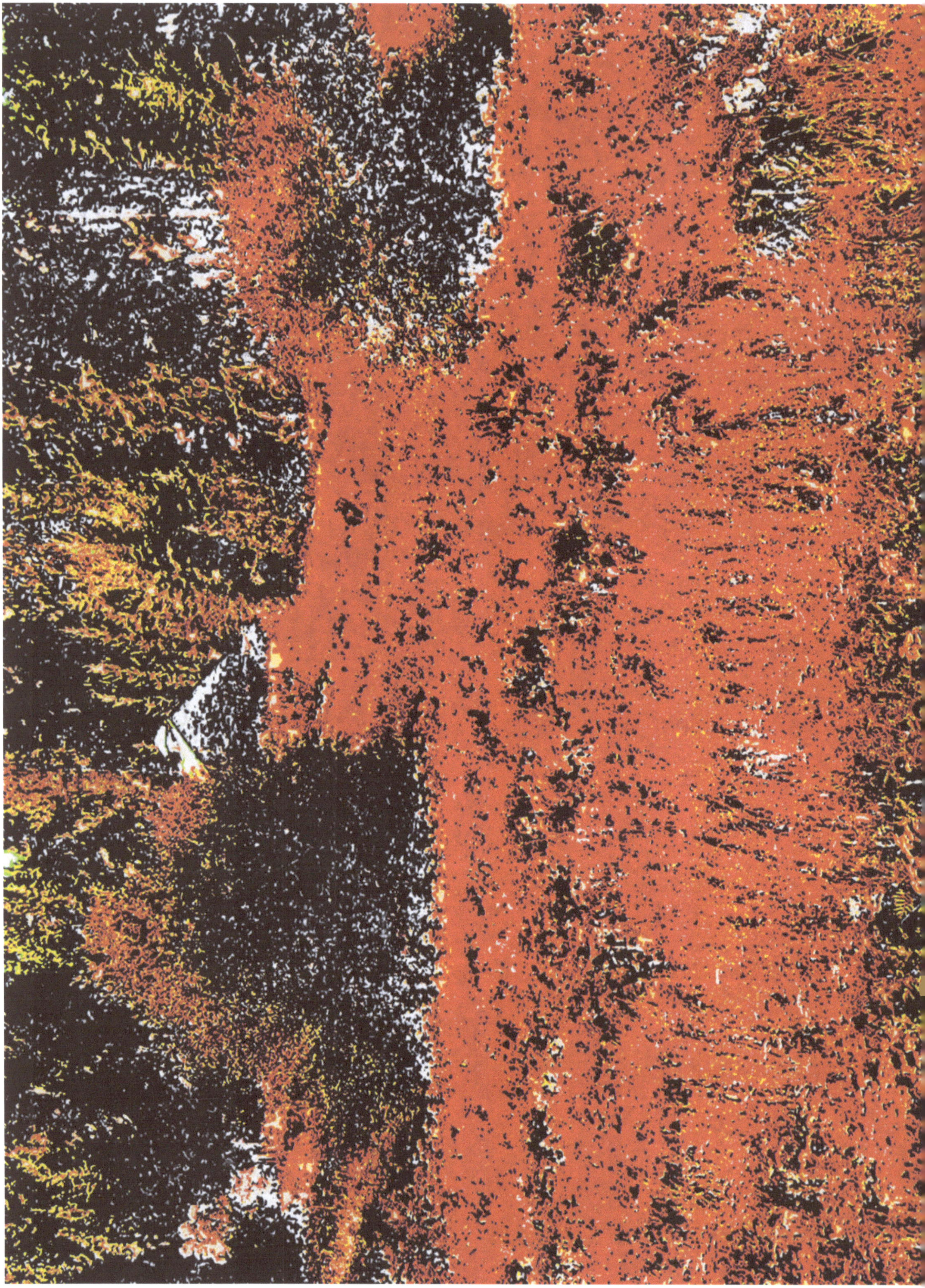

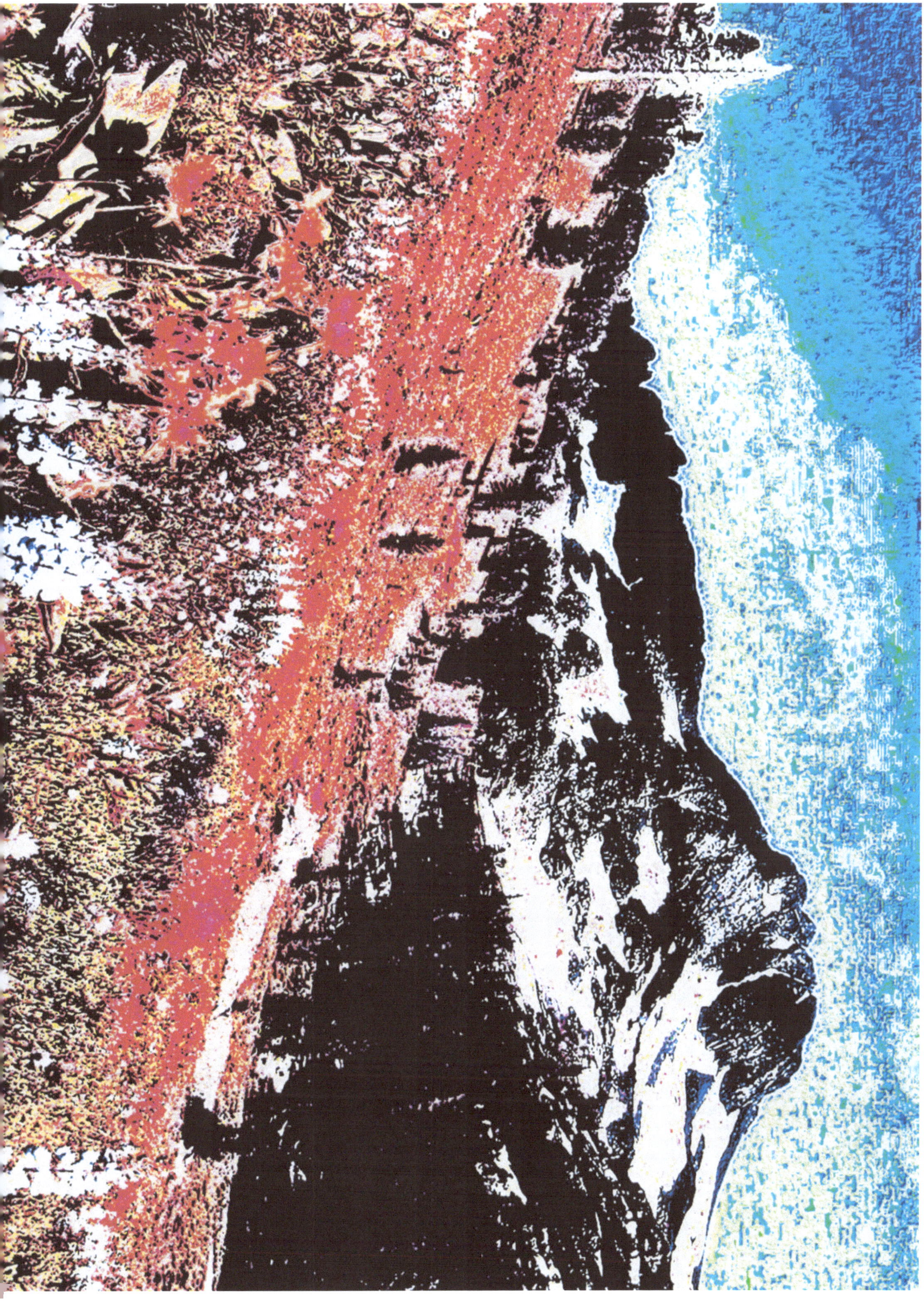

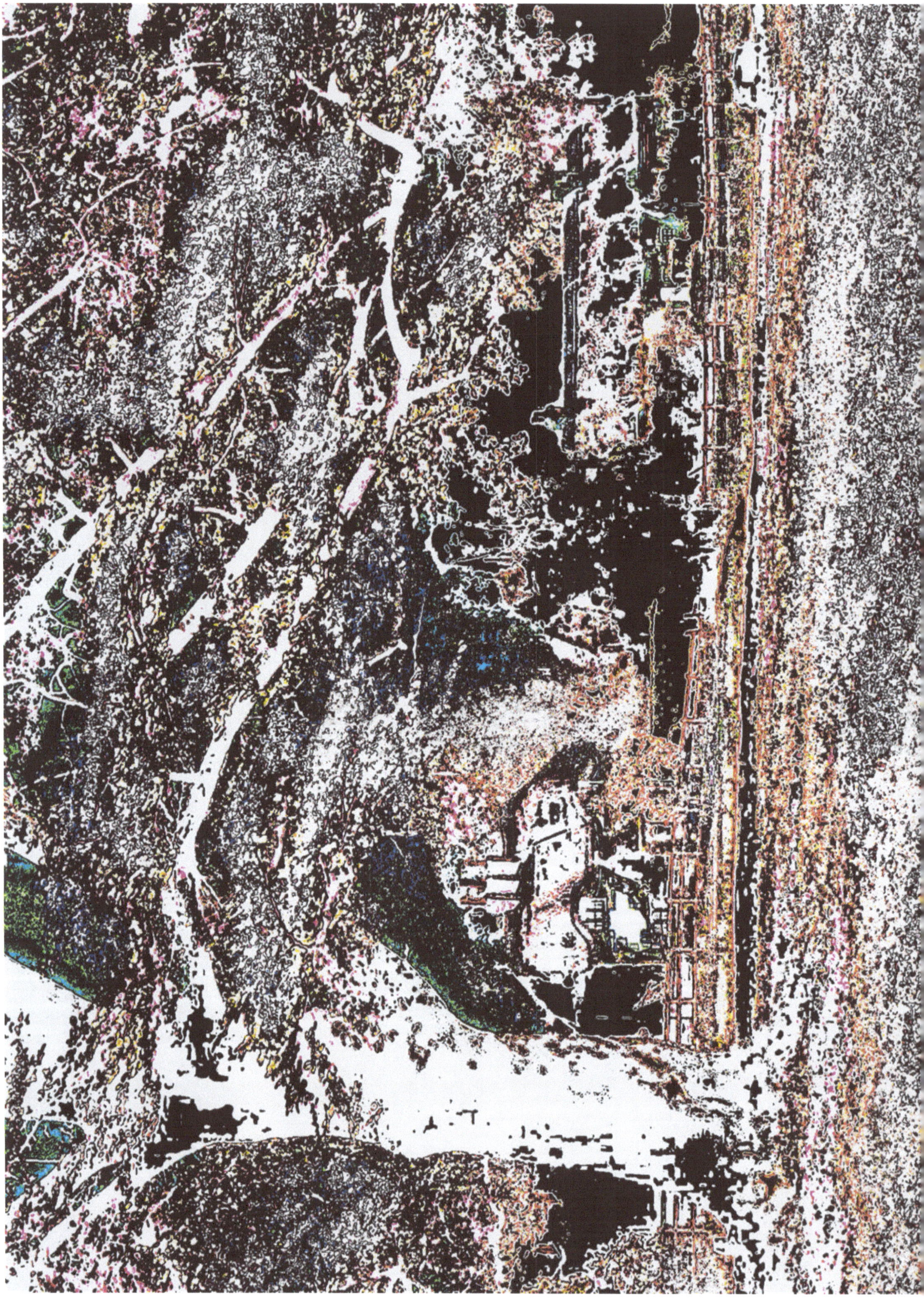

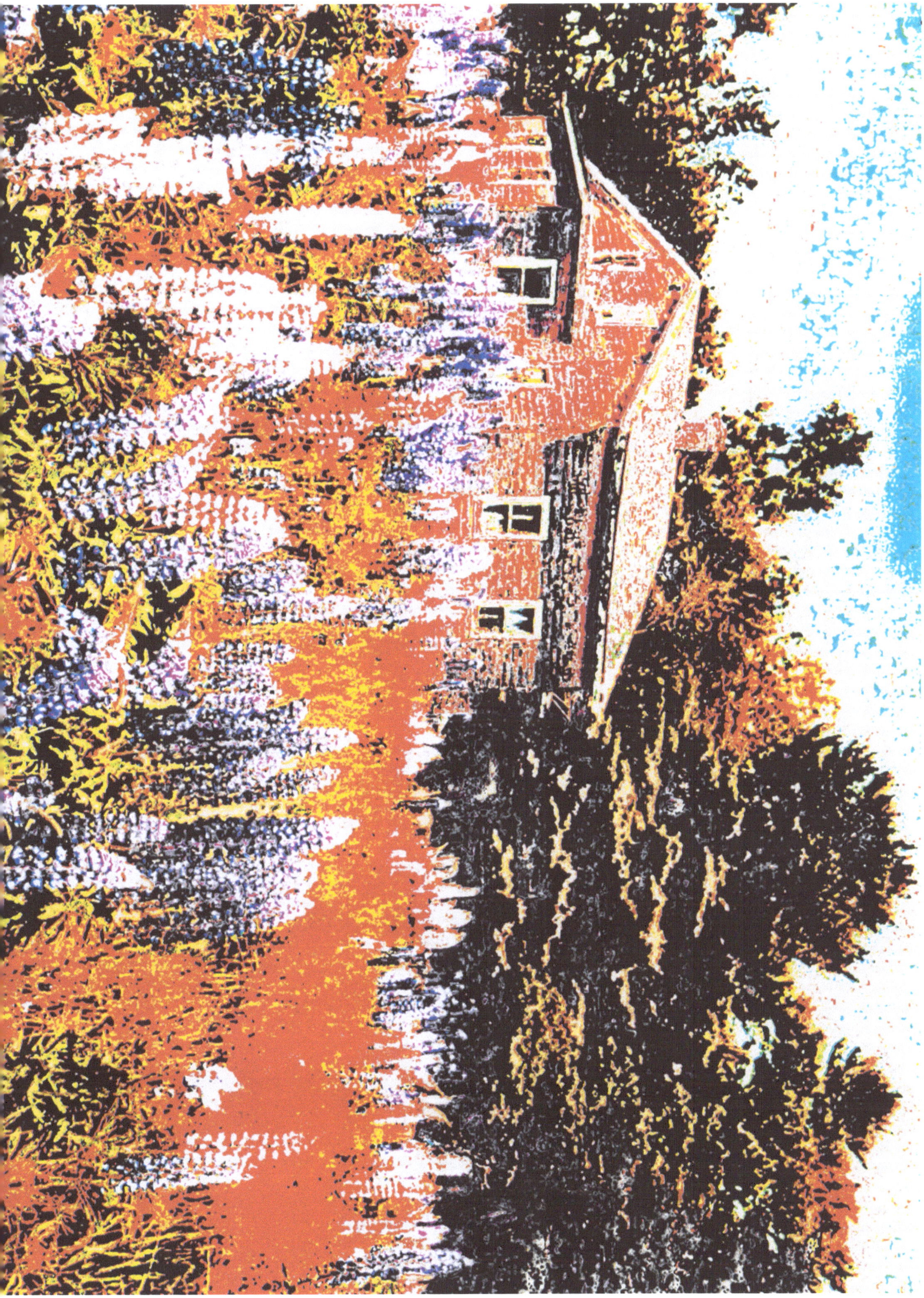

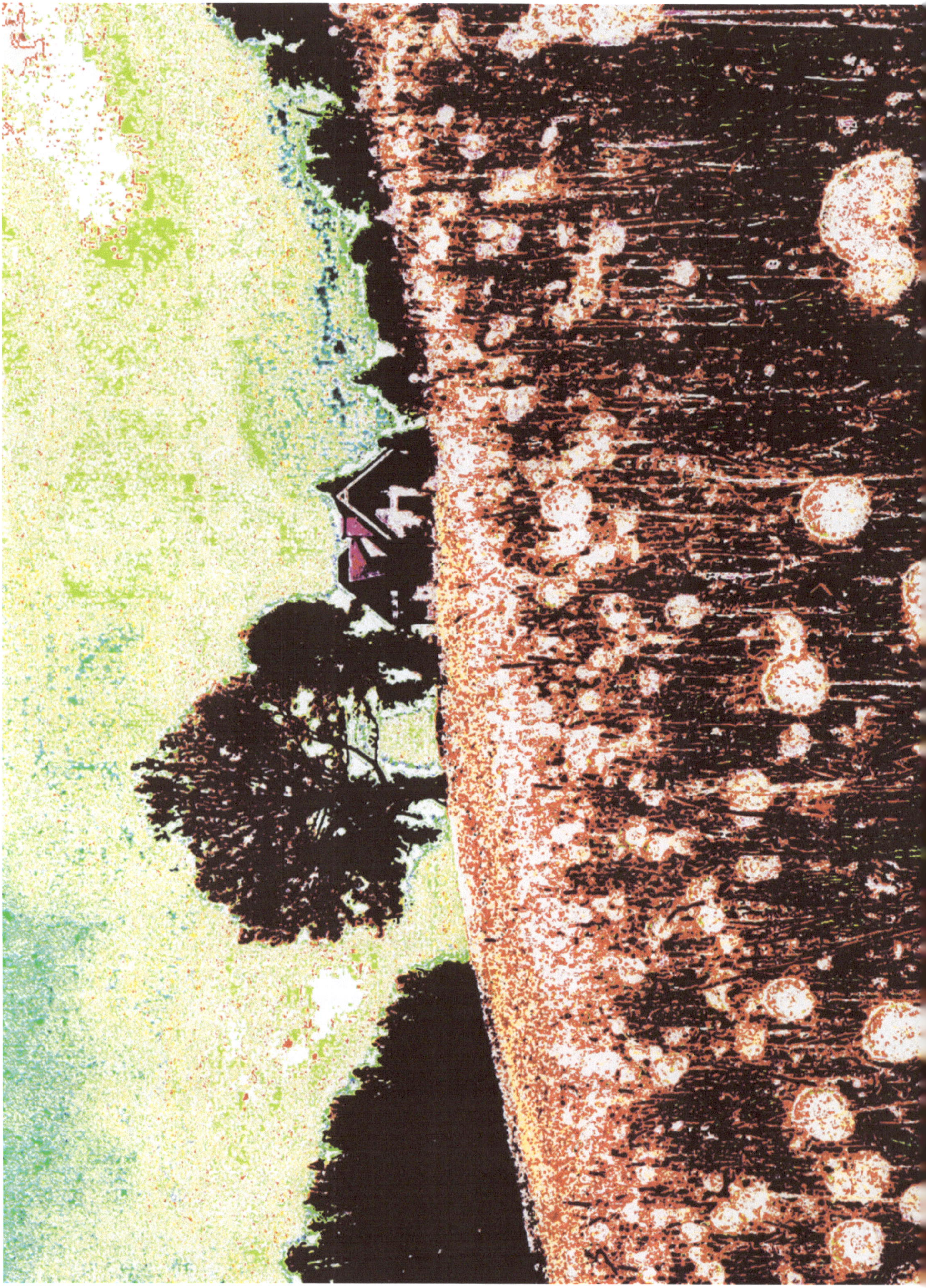

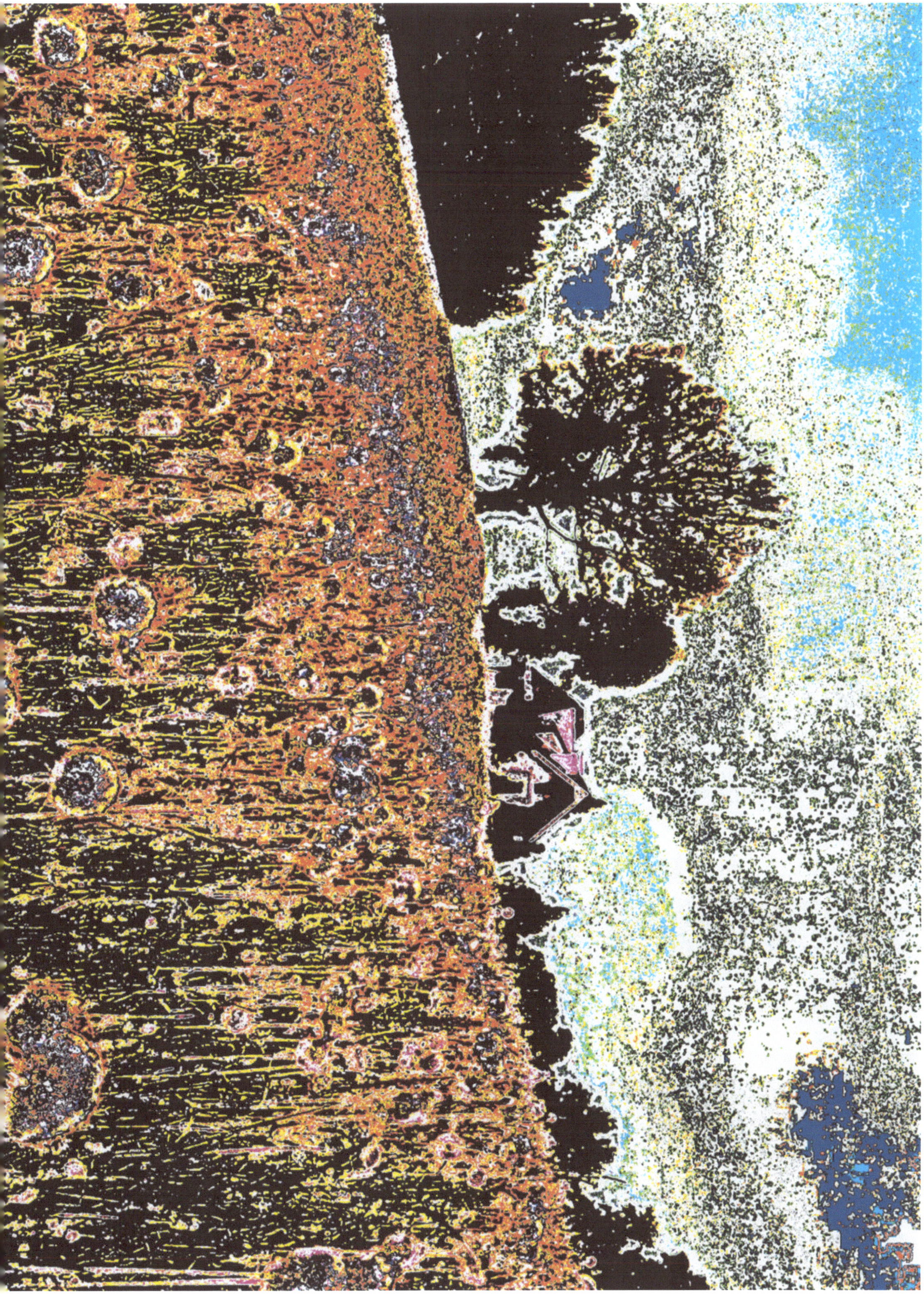

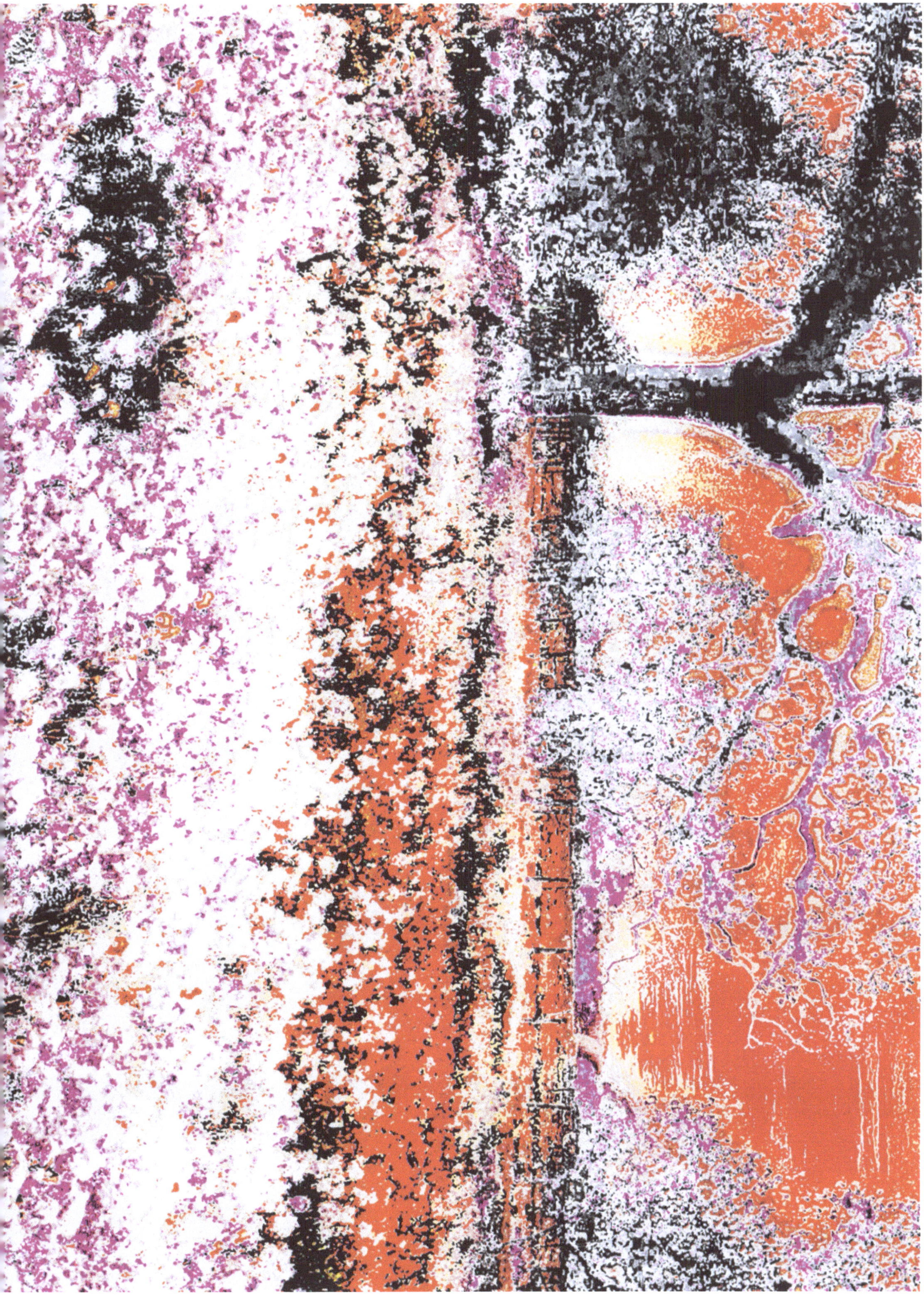

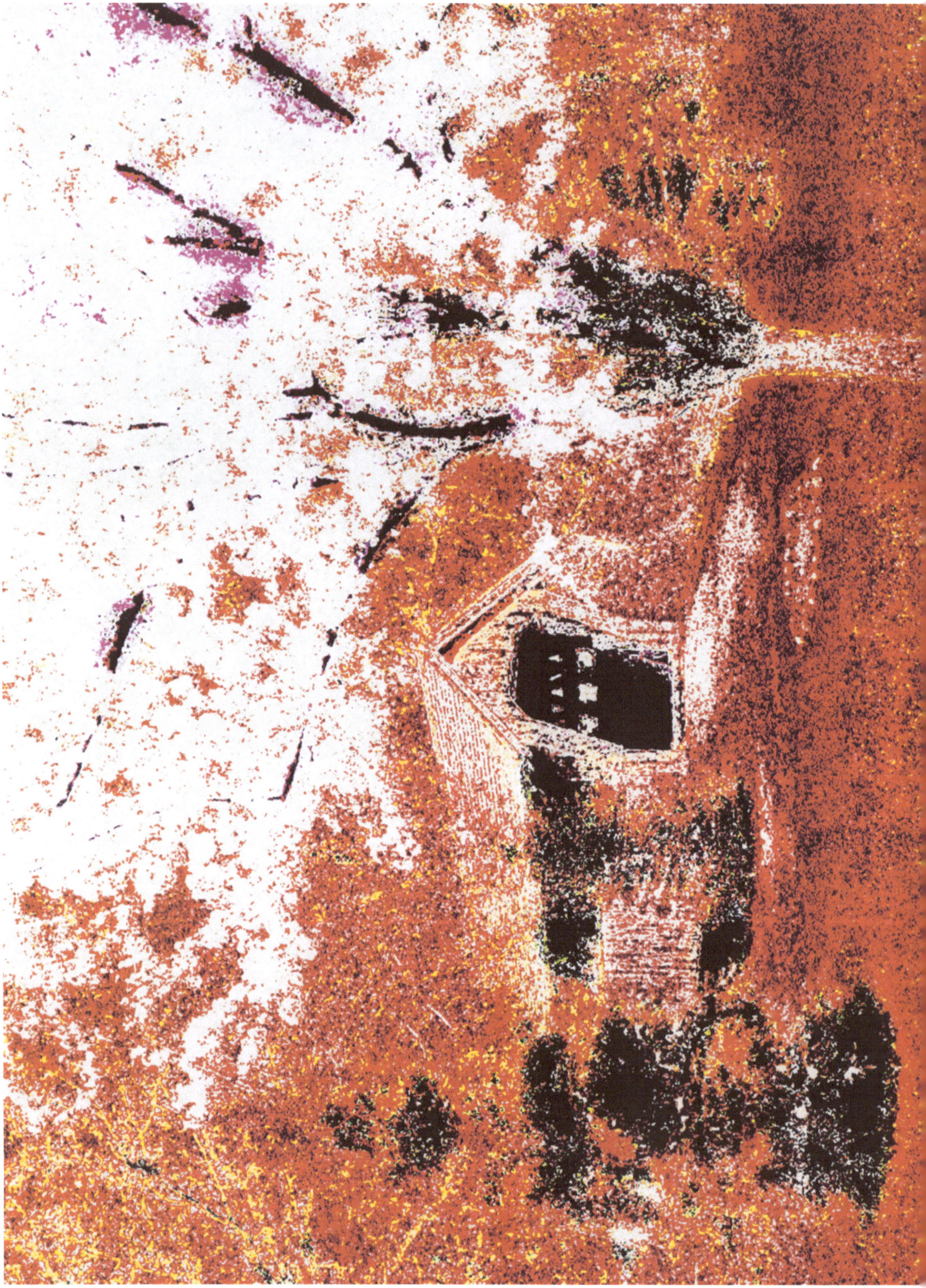

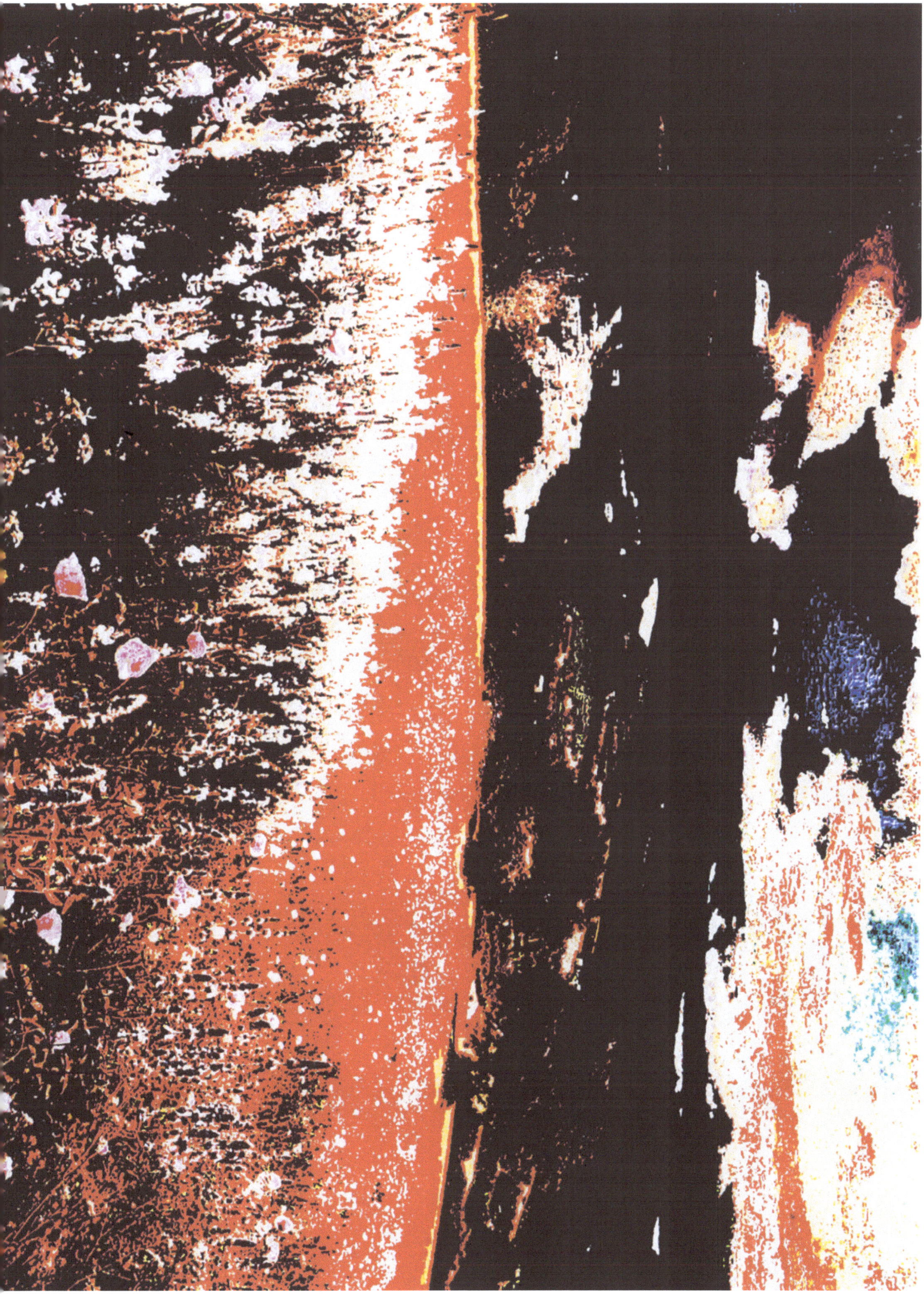

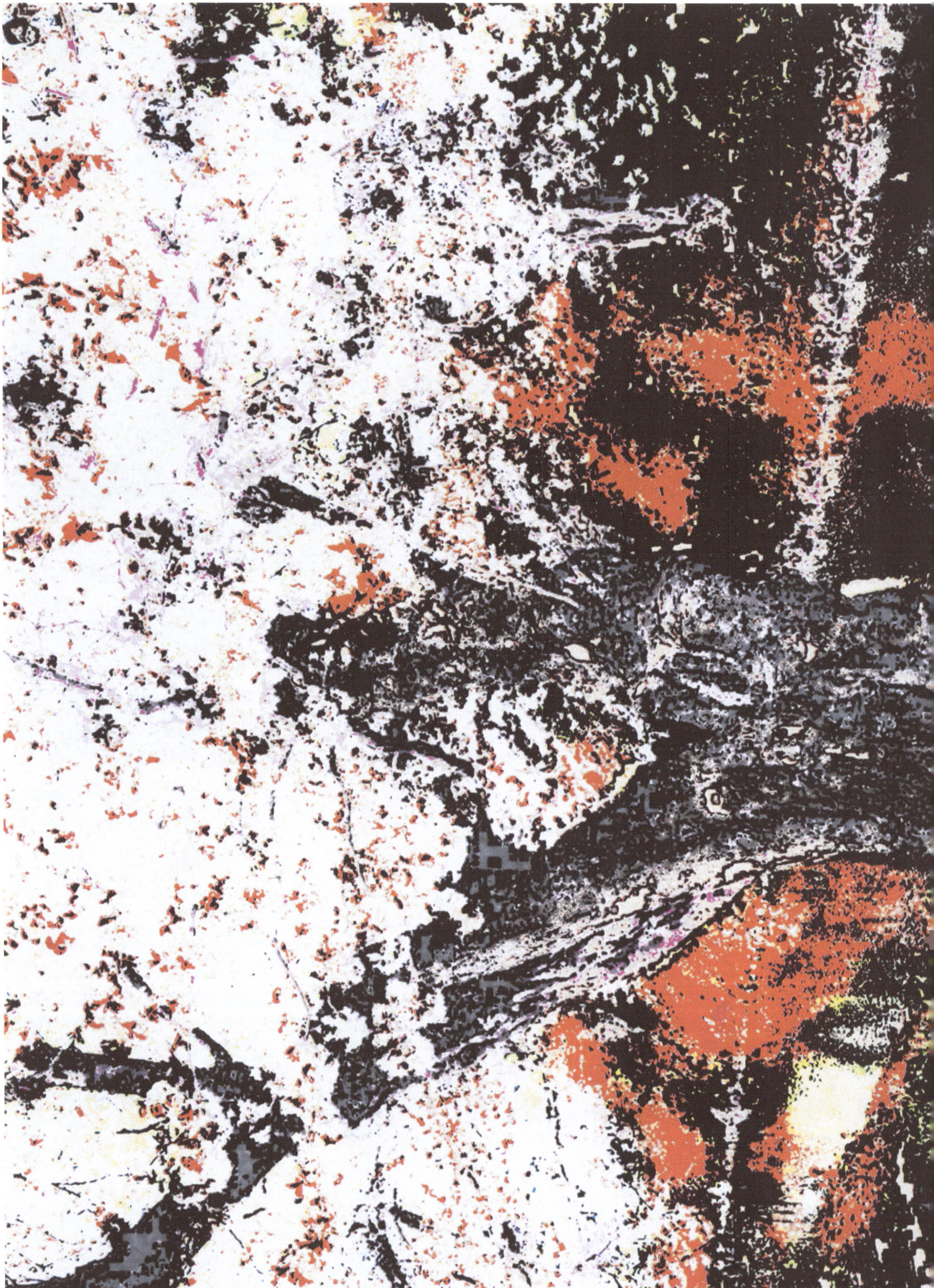

aggramatism - a condition in which speech production lacks grammatical structure and many function words and word endings are omitted

lexicalisation - the process of translating a words meaning into its sound representation during speech production

Homeostasis or homoeostasis (homeo- + -stasis) is the property of a system in which variables are regulated so that internal conditions remain stable and relatively constant. Examples of **homeostasis** include the regulation of temperature and the balance between acidity and alkalinity (pH).

di·as·po·ra

dīˈaspərə/

noun

noun: **diaspora**

1. Jews living outside Israel.
    - the dispersion of the Jews beyond Israel.
    - the dispersion of any people from their original homeland.
    - plural noun: **diasporas**
    - "the diaspora of boat people from Asia"
    - the people so dispersed.
    - "the Ukrainian diaspora flocked back to Kiev

su·per·la·tive

səˈpərlədiv/

adjective

1. **1.**
    2. of the highest quality or degree.
    3. "a superlative piece of skill"
    4. 5. excellent, magnificent, wonderful, marvelous, supreme, consummate,outstanding, remarkable, fine, choice, first-rate, first-class, premier,prime, unsurpassed, unequaled, unparalleled, unrivaled, preeminent;More

    6.

        8.

hīˈpərbəlē/

noun

1. exaggerated statements or claims not meant to be taken literally.
2. *synonyms:*
3. exaggeration, overstatement, magnification, embroidery, embellishment,excess, overkill, rhetoric; More

ex·tant

ˈekstənt,ekˈstant/

adjective

adjective: **extant**

1. (especially of a document) still in existence; surviving.
2. "the original manuscript is no longer extant"
3. *synonyms:*
4. still existing, in existence, existent, surviving, remaining, undestroyed
5. "extant manuscripts"

Origin

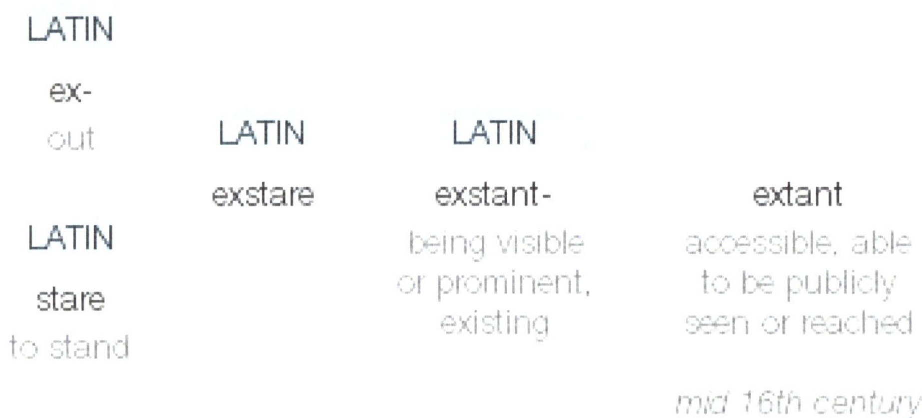

mid 16th century (in the sense ‘accessible, able to be publicly seen or reached’): from Latin *exstant-* ‘being visible or prominent, existing,’ from the verb *exstare*, from *ex-* ‘out’ + *stare* ‘to stand.’

see[1]

sē/

he who swims against the stream reaches the source

chuang tzu
taoism

repose, tranquility, stillness, inaction
when water is still, it is like a mirror, reflecting the beard and the eyebrows, and if water thus derives lucidly from stillness, how much more the faculties of the mind? the mind of the sage being in repose becomes the mirror of the universe, the speculum of all creation

the hidden unity of opposites and the dumb monkeys
viewed from the standpoint of Tao, a beam and pillar are identical. so are ugliness and beauty, greatness, wickedness, perverseness and strangeness... nothing is subject to either construction or to destruction, for these conditions are brought together into one. only the truly intelligent understand this principle of the identity of all things. they do not view things as apprehended by themselves, subjectively' but transfer themselves into the position of the things viewed. so it is that to place oneself in subjective relation to externals. - without consciousness of their objectivity- this is tao. but to wear out ones intellect in an obstinate adherence to the individuality of things, not recognizing the fact that all things are one - this is called three in the morning.

yet who shall say which is the correct standard of beauty? in my opinion, the standard of human virtue, and of positive and negative, is so obscured that it is impossible to know it as such

chatte poilue
creampie en la officina

sarraf.com

He emerged with a key insight: that in order to make sense of the perennial philosophical questions one has to step back and look at the mind itself, to see the mind as a tool; to look at how thought is structured and limited; to be weary of how our concepts influence our conclusions. He is like the first fish who said "hey, I just realized there is this thing I will call Water..." One fascinating question, which I will take up in another essay, is why it took so long, until 1781, for Western Philosophy to generate this perspective. From this starting point Kant developed a body of work, highly regarded to this day, that synthesized earlier views. He affirmed the Empiricist preoccupation with sense experience and the material world, but reconciled this with the Rationalist tradition by noting that experience itself is made possible only through deeper underlying ("a-priori") mental structures (deeper than concepts or ideas) such as space, time, and mathematical forms like numbers and shapes, that exist regardless of what exists in the material word.

delusions, religion, politics and economics - anthropology? 15
idea categorization and sorting significant information 15
contributions to understanding truth? 1 (doesn't make much sense)

points on religion: 7
1 deliberative vs instinctual ideas and decisions
1 cognition vs emotion with religious ideas
2 different categories of religious ideas
2 reality vs delusions with religious ideas
2 the holy spirit and a division of power with the trinity and government
3 the ultimate reality and pain and pleasure
4 the definitions of value and religious ideas and politics
2 mental constructs and delusions
3 different types of reality and religion and religious ideas
0 recategorizing religious stuff into a more practical or concise ideology
5 delusions or religious belief being unconscious
5 unconsciousness impacting how religion is felt or practiced (and its influence on ideas)
0 is god delusional? are other beliefs delusional? does that bias a viewpoint?
0 ideas or messages in a religion being communicated through religious practices
6 can kindness or other values be viewed with different consciousness?
6 is consciousness subjective and related to religious belief?

support for religion points: 2
government policies are like religious beliefs
reward and punishment system being simple in prehistoric times
physical reality being different from emotional reality and the spirit
personal qualities or 'interglobal' qualities relating to religion
history of religions relating messages

points on consciousness: 4
'reflective feelings'
mental representations being understandings or concepts
single emotions instead of multiple emotions and consciousness
expanded on delusions and cognition
the definition of words and consciousness and unconsciousness
meta-awareness and reflection
different types of consciousness and representations
physical processing and emotional processing are related
emotions and thoughts tie in with intellect and interact
intellect and emotion can absorb over time differently
mental representations and beliefs and desires

points about truth and reality (small articles): 8

people being emotional is subjective
reality involves understanding human motivation
mental models and associations are abstractions
conscious and unconscious determining attention
consciousness and unconsciousness determining who someone is and the will and the spirit (the minds comprehension)
experiential and physical tied in with understanding and intellect (deliberate and intelligent consciousness) (connecting it with 'teaching' sentences)
my amusing thoughts and feelings in the mind article - the only thing matters is feelings and 'thoughts' are useless
thinking provides humans with a more advanced way of viewing the world and people have different emotional interests
feelings can describe other feelings and can be physical or surreal

phenomenology and reality (final article): 2
reality and emotions, consciousness and vision linked with feelings

unique points in articles:

people being emotional is subjective
mental models and associations are abstractions
reality and emotions, consciousness and vision linked with feelings
feelings can describe other feelings and can be physical or surreal
'reflective feelings'
mental representations being understandings or concepts
single emotions instead of multiple emotions and consciousness
expanded on delusions and cognition

consciousness has many processes, such as vision and levels of attention, levels of feeling and thought
conscious processes also relate to unconscious processes
can people pay unconscious attention to something? can people direct their attention completely? - it obviously isn't completely under their control and involves many unconscious influences.
what plays a role with man and reality?
commonsense conception of action and consciousness
heidegger - what is the function of objects? can they be manipulated? (subjective experience towards objects) "aboutness" mental content is directed toward an object under an aspect
heidegger - if the going gets difficult, switch to subject/object intentionality

In their self-enclosed, peripheral fields of inquiry, which focus mainly on human relations within the lifeworld, phenomenological investigations today innovate and greatly enrich our common culture. Yet when it comes to our philosophical probing into the real, they float unattached to the great lines of phenomenological inquiry. - Anna-Teresa Tymieniecka - **Does the World Exist?: Plurisignificant Ciphering of Reality (Analecta Husserliana)**

Human Creation Between Reality and Illusion (Analecta Husserliana) edited by Anna-Teresa Tymieniecka - by lawrence kimmel -

parmenides was quoted by heidegger "to know one singular thing we have to know all things"

How powerful and significant is the unconscious mind?

The Phenomenological Realism of the Possible Worlds:

The 'A Priori', Activity and Passivity of Consciousness, Phenomenology and Nature Papers and Debate of the Second International Conference Held by the International Husserl and Phenomenological Research Society New York, N. Y., September 4–9, 1972 **(Analecta Husserliana)**

edited by Anna-Teresa Tymieniecka

Anna-Teresa Tymieniecka / Imaginatio Creatrix: the creative versus the constitutive function of man, and the possible worlds

Human being appears as the major dynamic factor within this system not only with the respect to the progress onwards but also at the level of introducing the essential and basic level of

www.ingramcontent.com/pod-product-compliance
Lightning Source LLC
LaVergne TN
LVHW070955210926
848482LV00002B/217